Broken Clay

*Finding Renewal in
the Potter's Hands*

a memoir

Tika McCoy

979-8-9885744-4-6 Paperback
979-8-9885744-3-9 Hardback
979-8-9885744-5-3 eBook

For my parents, Willie and Earline Lockhart

For my parents, Willie and Earline Lockhart

CONTENTS

NOTE FROM TIKA

Welcome to *Broken Clay: Finding Renewal in the Potter's Hands*. I'm thrilled that you decided to join me on this journey of Christian renewal after brokenness. I wasn't always broken. The first forty years of my life were uneventful. My parents provided a safe and comfortable lifestyle for me. I reaped the benefits of that comfort and enjoyed my childhood and adolescence. After a carefree life of living with my parents, I set out to achieve the "American Dream." I married, bought a house, started a career, acquired debt, and traveled. My life was good. I had no complaints. Then, without warning, life happened. Ill-prepared to handle the hardships that came my way, my life spiraled out of control. It broke me and shattered me into pieces. Yet, the loving and gracious God we serve put me back together and reshaped me into a woman of Christ. Even though I left the faith more times than I can count, God never gave up on me.

In my youth, I attended church with my aunt, sister-in-law, and grandmother. Once I entered junior high school, my focus shifted to spending more time with friends and I stopped attending church. In my twenties, as I started to build my adult life, I joined a church, but after drama unfolded, I stopped attending yet again.

When I needed God and came crawling back in my forties, He welcomed me with open arms. What an amazing God we serve! I couldn't keep the news of His acceptance, love, and grace to myself. You're holding my testimony of God's amazing grace and how He sustained me through my tribulations. If you are in a place of brokenness, I pray that this book will be a source of inspiration for you. God put me back together. And, He will do the same for you!

May God keep and bless you, Tika.

"But now, Lord, You are our Father; we are the clay,
and You our potter, and all of us are the work of Your hand."

. . .

ISAIAH 64:8

HOW TO NAVIGATE THIS BOOK

This is a working memoir. After reading my story, you will have the opportunity to consider your own story. Each chapter of the memoir will begin with a personal story of a storm I faced. I'll share details of how I struggled without God at the center of my life. I reference Bible verses throughout my story using the *New American Standard Bible* (NASB) translation. Some verses highlight biblical insight I wish I had known during my storm. Other verses focus on biblical knowledge I learned on my faith journey.

The life application section is all about you. Complete the chapter discussion questions to consider how you might respond in a similar situation. After the discussion questions, read the Bible story to draw inspiration and strength from God's infallible Word and remember how God is the same yesterday, today, and forever. Lastly, answer the personal reflection questions as you consider your own story.

Healing takes time, and what worked for me may be different for you, and that's okay. The key is to recognize how God sustains *you* during *your* storm. I pray that you will realize God's presence on your faith journey.

INTRODUCTION

"When it rains, it pours."
"Tragedy happens in threes."
"If it isn't one thing, it's another."
"Life happens."

When I reflected on the hardships I have faced, these common sayings came to mind. I imagine you also thought of your own life challenges as you read those sayings, especially if those challenges happened in quick succession.

No one is immune from life's ups and downs, and Christians are no exception. We're reminded of this in 1 Peter 4:12, "Beloved, do not be surprised at the fiery ordeal among you, which comes upon you for your testing, as though some strange thing were happening to you." While we're in the middle of life's struggles, like sickness, divorce, job loss, and grief, it's hard to recognize that God is working things out for our good, as stated in Romans 8:28. "And we know that God causes all things to work together for good to those who love God, to those who are called according to His purpose." Even faithful Christians need time to process and reflect that their pain is for the greater good of glorifying God.

As my faith matured, I gained a greater perspective of how God used my hardship for His means. This led me to share my sorrows to testify to God's loving embrace of me and how He sustained me even when I didn't realize it. Before gaining this understanding, many people, myself included, question why God allows pain and suffering. They often ask themselves why God hasn't intervened to save them from their hardships. For some, during these difficult times, their faith wanes, and they become bitter and even angry with God. I counted myself in that group at one time. I certainly was upset and mad at God during several trials in my life, and sometimes I stopped praying altogether. I refused to go to church. At my lowest, I thought, *"What is the point in revering God if He will not save me amid my trials?"* I needed answers and wanted to know why He didn't save me. I wondered if I had done something wrong to deserve my pain. I searched the Bible for answers and discovered that even the most influential people in the Bible suffered from unbearable hardships.

Paul suffered from a thorn in the flesh. Joseph's brothers sold him for twenty pieces of silver. David fled to the wilderness to escape Saul. Naomi grieved the deaths of her husband and sons. I can go on, but you get the idea. During their times of suffering and uncertainty, they had no way of knowing that their pain would lead to their spiritual growth and God's ultimate plan for their lives – and ours. Through the oral gospel traditions of their time, they knew of and worshipped the one true God, but I'm not sure if they knew their stories would one day be added to the canon of Scripture and be a source of inspiration thousands of years later.

During their trials, they had moments of weakness, and some even questioned God's motives. I found this comforting as it revealed their humanness. They cried out to God just as I did and wanted Him to swoop in and save them. Knowing this permitted me to be kinder to myself in my despair because even the people we study in the Bible had moments of despair. Perhaps you, too, are experiencing the uncertainty of the question, "Where is God?" in the midst of your divorce, loss, infidelity, pain, health crisis, etc. I want to encourage you to remain faithful to God's Word and seek out individuals with survival stories for spiritual encouragement.

Our faith and inspiration extend beyond the sixty-six books in the Bible. We also find inspiration in our lived experiences. Redemptive stories of God's grace give hope to people who struggle to manage their daily lives, including the raising a family, caring for elderly parents, managing grief, etc. As Christians, we are instructed to share the good news with others; in doing so, we should also share our testimony with them. One specific verse that speaks to this is Luke 8:39, "Return to your home and describe what great things God has done for you. So he went away, proclaiming throughout the city what great things Jesus had done for him." I'm excited to proclaim the great things Jesus has done for me!

My faith journey is not a linear story where I accepted Jesus as my Lord and Savior and immediately fell in line with Christian beliefs. I had to overcome the loss of loved ones, divorce, grief, infidelity, abuse, and anger issues to reach the point I am at today. My story is quite messy. As you journey through some of the most difficult moments in my life written in this book, you'll get a glimpse into the doubt, anger, pain, and spiritual weariness I felt. You will also see how these losses turned into my faith in Christ. I hope it is a source of inspiration to you as you navigate the challenges in your life.

CHAPTER 1

———

My Name Is Job

"Now on the day when his sons and his daughters were eating and
drinking wine in their oldest brother's house, a messenger came
to Job and said, the oxen were plowing and the female donkeys
feeding beside them, and the Sabeans attacked and took them.
They also killed the servants with the edge of the sword, and I
alone have escaped to tell you. While he was still speaking, another came and said, the fire of God fell from heaven and burned
up the sheep and the servants and consumed them, and I alone
have escaped to tell you. While he was still speaking, another
came and said, the Chaldeans formed three units and made a
raid on the camels and took them, and killed the servants with
the edge of the sword, and I alone have escaped to tell you."

. . .

JOB 1:13-17

I titled this chapter, "My Name is Job." By no means am I asserting that I am a just and righteous person of faith like Job. In fact, I'm fully aware that I am a sinner and not worthy of God's grace and mercy. Yet, Job's story spoke to me. Like me, many people who face hard life challenges turn to the book of Job to make sense of their own lives.

Job lost his children and possessions one after another, and his friends blamed him for the troubles in his life. His wife, tired of his lamentations, told him to curse God and die. Yet, through it all, Job remained faithful to God. Without God in my life, I struggled to manage what had become my tumultuous life. Today, I have a better understanding on how God sustained me while I suffered through death, infidelity, and abuse. But, while amid my own Job trials, I questioned God and often cried out, "Why me?"

Some days in my hopelessness, I believed I was the only one dealing with hardships. When I saw people and families out and about, they seemed happy and cheerful. I watched as they joyfully engaged with one another, and I couldn't imagine they had any struggles in their lives. It wasn't until a friend opened up to me over dinner about her life challenges that I began to see things differently.

We met at our favorite restaurant for dinner. Walking past the crowd waiting for a table, we made a beeline for the bar and quickened our steps to secure the last two remaining seats. I high-fived her in a victorious celebration of our luck. After settling in, she shared how she had questioned God after the finalization of her divorce. She wondered if there was a deeper meaning or lesson she needed to take from the dissolution of her marriage. I admitted I had similar thoughts about my tribulations. As our discussion continued, my mind replayed the images of the families I watched that I previously assumed had no drama or pain in their lives. I remembered all of the times I smiled and laughed in the presence of others as I masked my pain. No one knew the hurt I carried. Perhaps people also looked at me and assumed I had it together.

On my drive home from dinner, I acknowledged the reality that I wasn't the only one dealing with life challenges, and that, like others, I did an excellent job of hiding my trauma. It gave me a semblance of peace knowing that life happens and that it wasn't happening to just me – that I hadn't done anything wrong to cause my pain. I hope you feel peace knowing you are not alone as you read my story.

Sadly, tragedy and suffering are universal, but how we respond to our suffering is not. I learned this when studying the trials Job endured. Job, whom the Bible describes as blameless and upright, remained faithful to God when faced with grief and loss. Job continued to worship God in his pain. My husband and I were not as upright and righteous as Job. Instead of worshipping God like Job, we engaged in destructive behaviors in response to our suffering. My husband abused alcohol and had an affair when faced with grief and loss, while I struggled to manage my emotions. We didn't have a solid foundation to help us manage the suffering we experienced.

Jerry and I attended church early in our marriage. We enjoyed listening to the sermons and the music. Unfortunately, we never developed an understanding of the Bible that was needed to direct our lives, and sadly, we didn't have a solid Christian faith to lean on when life got hard. This was evident when we left the church after our pastor was removed due to accusations of inappropriate relationships. Young and disillusioned, we threw up our hands in despair. We never waited for new leadership to right the ship or share a new church vision. Like every American city, our hometown had plenty of churches we could've joined. We were so hurt by the actions of our pastor, the pastor who married us, that we decided against finding a new church. We walked away and never looked back. I can't help but wonder how things may have differed in our marriage if we'd had a God-centered faith to lean on.

The first bout of tragedy struck when Jerry and I had been happily married for sixteen years, and his mother died unexpectedly. While the loss of a parent is unbearable, this loss was especially devastating because his mother didn't raise him. In his grief, he shared with me, "I never really got to have a relationship with her."

Not only did he lose her, but he also lost the dream he longed for in a mother-son relationship. He had made every attempt to build a relationship with her. Even though the relationship didn't materialize as he had hoped, it wasn't due to his lack of effort.

For a short time, his mother lived in Detroit, about three hours from where we lived. He reached out to her for holiday plans, and she often invited us to spend the 4th of July, Thanksgiving, or other holidays there with her. We packed our bags for the long holiday weekend and always had a great time. When she died, Jerry mourned her, and he lamented what their relationship could have been. We certainly did not have a perfect marriage, but after the death of his mother, I noticed changes in Jerry's behavior, which negatively impacted our marriage.

One night, he had come home late from work. I heard him open the garage door and made my way to the kitchen to meet him. Stringent grainy scents of carrots, caramel, and musk engulfed him. With my nostril full of the aroma, I suspiciously asked, "Jerry, have you been drinking?"

"I had a couple after work. I know you're not talking. You always drink."

I sighed in agreement. When we dined out, he ordered a Coke, and I ordered a glass of white wine or a mixed cocktail. Even at home, he had pop, while I usually drank an adult beverage.

"Yeah, but..." I stopped mid-sentence, realizing it wasn't the time to defend myself. Instead, I asked, "Are you okay?"

His family had a history of alcohol and drug abuse, so he abstained from all substances out of fear of becoming addicted. I admired his control, especially at outings or family events where everyone else had a beer or two. I often commended him for his convictions on abstaining from alcohol, and he jokingly ribbed me for the opposite and we had some great laughs. Yet, we didn't laugh when Jerry started drinking. His alcohol consumption took him down a dark path as he tried to mask the pain of losing his mother.

In contrast, when Job learned that a great wind had struck his son's house and killed his children, he worshipped God. Job 1:20 reads, "Then Job arose and tore his robe and shaved his head, and he fell to the ground and worshiped. He said, 'Naked I came from my mother's womb, and naked I shall return there. The Lord gave and the Lord has taken away.'" Job understood that everyone and everything belongs to God. In his grief, he managed to thank the Lord for what He provided and also thanked God when He took it away. Not only did Job lose his children, but he also lost his livestock and was afflicted with boils on his skin. Yet he remained faithful to the Lord through it all. I wish Jerry and I would have remained faithful.

Like Job, Jerry had multiple losses. And, like Job, he didn't have time to process the first loss before the second one took his breath away. Jerry's grandmother, his rock, died six months after his mother died. Losing his grandmother devastated him. She had adopted Jerry when he was a child, and they were extremely close.

When she aged and needed care, she asked Jerry to take on primary duties over her natural-born children. Jerry agreed without giving it a second thought. He enjoyed caring for her. He took her to doctor visits, helped with her medication, and found a rehabilitation facility when she needed post-cardiac arrest assistance. He loved caring for her.

When Jerry's mother died, he shared how he had never gotten to know her. When his grandmother died, he was silent. He had no words to describe what he felt. Bereft, his alcohol consumption increased to the point of no return.

Having a "couple" after work turned into going to a local dive bar on the weekend with his "boys." Suddenly, his nights were spent hanging out more and more with guys he referred to as his boys. I didn't know anything about them or who they were. I asked, "Who are you going out with again?" He offered little details outside of "my boys from work." This wasn't like him at all. Sensing this wasn't the best crowd for him to be around, I warned him to be wary of his drinking and new friends. I worried his so-called "friends" were not helping to pull him out of the pit of grief he had found himself. In fact, I believed they were pulling him down even further.

Supportive friends often help us to navigate through our challenges. Looking to Job's friends, who certainly weren't perfect, they at least challenged him with questions and profound statements, which ultimately led to Job's greater reverence for God. In Job 2:13, we learn that Job's friends sat silently with him for seven days. The verse states, "Then they sat down on the ground with him for seven days and seven nights with no one speaking a word to him, for they saw that his pain was great." They allowed Job to grieve and comforted him through their presence. This is the type of response that a friend should have when one is going through a tragedy.

I don't believe Jerry's "boys" had the caliber of Job's friends. Instead of sitting with him in his pain, they supported him in his efforts to numb it. His "boys" didn't come to our house to sit quietly with him when his mom or grandmother passed. Instead, Jerry spent time with them away from our home, away from me, at a bar getting drunk.

After seven days of quietly sitting, Job's friends began to challenge him. I've read commentaries debating whether Job's friends were more harmful than helpful. Job 20:5 stands out, "That the triumphing of the wicked is short, and the joy of the godless momentary." Job's friend, Zophar, called him wicked and godless. This is undoubtedly an awful thing for a friend to say, yet as Job's friends continued with similar statements, it allowed Job to defend himself and God. They put Job in a position to uphold his character and to proclaim that God is just in His actions. True friends should challenge us to think and process the situations in which we find ourselves. Of course, Job's friends could have been kinder in their words, but through their criticisms, Job defended God.

I wished Jerry's new friends had confronted him and asked tough questions to challenge his behavior. I don't know if any of those individuals lived miserable existences, but as the saying goes, "misery loves company." I can't say for certain, but they appeared to encourage his excessive drinking. I'm not sure they wanted the best for him. 1 Corinthians 15:33 says, "Do not be deceived, bad company corrupts good morals." This verse may also explain why Jerry didn't spend time with his lifelong friends who knew why he abstained from alcohol.

His childhood friends certainly would have called his harmful behavior to his attention. I get the sense he turned his back on those of us who would have helped him. When I tried to intervene, he refused my offer of help. I encouraged him to speak with family members, hoping they could offer the support I couldn't. It broke my heart when I saw the pain and despair on his face and the dull and distant look in his eyes. I wanted him to get help. The Jerry I once knew was gone.

Like a broken record, I begged Jerry to get help. Exasperated, he yelled that he was fine and told me to drop the conversation. Then, I learned why he didn't want or need my support. He found comfort and support in another woman. I don't know which came first, the drinking or the affair. Everything happened so fast. In practically a blink of an eye, we went from a happy marriage preparing to expand our family through adoption to a life where we were both in the throes of sin.

I marvel that Job never lost his faith, no matter what he suffered. Job 1:22, "Through all this Job did not sin nor did he blame God." Sin seemed to be the only option for Jerry and me.

I struggled to manage my emotions. Quick to anger, I yelled and screamed at Jerry about his drinking and infidelity. The smallest infraction filled me with sadness and anxiety. I cried uncontrollably and descended into bouts of depression. In my sorrowful state, I made one of the hardest decisions of my life and I grieved my last hope of ever becoming a mother.

The anguish I felt when the realization set in that mother would never be one of my titles broke me. I avoided walking anywhere near the baby aisle at groceries stores. Before, I spent hours walking the aisles browsing baby clothes and supplies I needed and wanted for the nursery I had decorated in a brown and green monkey theme. Sadly, I never got the opportunity to use that nursery.

On a particularly emotional and stressful day, I searched my cell phone contact list until I reached my adoption social worker's number. I tried to not visualize the nursery across the hall from my bedroom. I was unsuccessful. "Ring," I thought about the playful monkey crib bumper. "Ring," and the Britax car seat I had spent hours researching. "Ring," then there were those decorative reusable cloth diapers I'd ordered. "Ring," and finally, the cute little panda book I wrote that would be the baby's personal adoption story. By the time the call went to voicemail, I was inconsolable. I heard the beep, sighed, and barely squeaked, "This is Tika Frances; I need to close our file. Jerry and I won't be seeking to adopt at this time. Thank you, bye."

I grasped at my heart, spastic beats constricted and lessened until it caught the rhythm of the void I would forever carry in my heart. Broken, I crawled into bed and screamed in agony. When Jerry came home later that night, I cried as I told him I had closed our adoption file. He stared at me, then asked if I had really closed the file. Defiant, I folded my arms across my chest. I prepared for the argument I was sure we were about to have. He continued to stare before walking away and murmuring under his breath how I hadn't discussed the status of our adoption with him.

He had reason to be upset with me. I decided without conferring with him. Jerry and I were a mess, and rarely did a day pass without us arguing and yelling at one another. Knowing how destructive our lives had become, I couldn't bring a baby into our home. Broken. I wanted what my parents had, children, birthday parties, family road trips, and opening gifts on Christmas mornings. Accepting that this would never happen for me, I wanted to be held and comforted by my husband, but Jerry couldn't meet my needs. He struggled to manage his own pain, and he didn't have the emotional capacity to help me. Things had gotten so bad that we were incapable of caring for and being kind to one another.

In contrast, Job demonstrated how to care for others under all circumstances. In a selfless act of love for his family, Job offered a burnt sacrifice on behalf of his children. The burnt offering signified an atonement for sin, acknowledgment of wrongdoing, and a prayer for compassion from God.

Job 1:5, "When the days of feasting had completed their cycle, Job would send word to them and consecrate them, getting up early in the morning and offering burnt offerings according to the number of them all; for Job said, perhaps my sons have sinned and cursed God in their hearts. Job did so continually." Job was so devoted to God and cared so much for his children that offering a burnt offering on their behalf came naturally to him. Unfortunately, Jerry and I didn't have the wherewithal to offer that level of love and support for one another, much less pray. Without prayer, support, and love, we continued to spiral downward.

As if things couldn't get any worse, I noticed Jerry's paychecks weren't being deposited into our joint account. We struggled without his income, so I relentlessly questioned him for answers. He tried to convince me, that a payroll error caused the discrepancy. I refused to accept his excuse, and he finally admitted he had gotten fired from his job.

At the admission of losing his job, I reacted similarly to Job's wife, and I wasn't kind to him. Job 2:9, "Then his wife said to him, do you still hold fast your integrity? Curse God and die." She lashed out to him to stop defending God and for him to die already. Job's wife grew tired of his faith and admonished him for it.

Similar to Job's wife, I grew tired of Jerry, but for a different reason. She was tired of Job's faith in God, and I was tired of Jerry's behavior and constant lies. I yelled at him when he admitted to being fired from his job. My words dripping with disdain, I tore into him that his drinking, affair, and combative attitude were to blame. I even went as far as to say he deserved to be fired. I lost my patience with Jerry and offered no words of comfort.

In my mind, all of our problems were due to his actions. I no longer cared about or tried to solve his drinking problem. I stopped trying to comfort him in his grief. Anger and rage consumed me. I was so busy blaming Jerry for his destructive behaviors that I failed to recognize how my anger led me down a path to my destruction. Then it would only be a matter of time until I found myself in a situation I never imagined would happen to me in a million years.

LIFE APPLICATION
Chapter Discussion Questions

1. Sadly, tragedy and suffering are universal, but our response to suffering is not. Job, whom the Bible describes as blameless and upright, remained faithful to God when faced with grief and loss. Job continued to worship God in his pain. **How (have/do) you respond to suffering and pain in your life?**

2. We all need supportive friends to help us navigate through our challenges. Looking to Job's friends, who certainly weren't perfect, they at least challenged him with questions and profound statements, which ultimately led to Job's greater reverence for God. **How would you compare your family and friends to Job's friends?**

3. The support we receive from family and friends during life's storms is invaluable. However, not all family and friends can provide the emotional or spiritual support we require on our healing journey. Read Job 2:11-13. **How would you describe how your family and friends respond to you amid your troubles?**

4. Today, when I study Job, I have a greater perspective on how God sustained me while I suffered through death, infidelity, and abuse. However, before I acquired that perspective, I questioned God. Our faith journeys can be long and messy. **Where are you on your faith journey? Do you question or blame God for your pain? Do you have a greater perspective on how God uses suffering in our lives?**

5. Job shows how we can perform a selfless act of caring for others while living our own lives. Job offered a burnt sacrifice on behalf of his children. He said perhaps they sinned and cursed God in their

hearts. Today, this is as simple as praying for our loved ones who have probably sinned and cursed God. **What selfless acts do you perform to demonstrate how you care for others, even while dealing with what life may throw your way?**

BIBLE STORY

While reading my story, I imagine you thought of your own Job trial(s). Perhaps your trials happened years ago, or you're in the middle of one right now, or one is just starting. It is undoubtedly painful, and you may even feel overwhelmed and depressed. I want to encourage you that you're not alone in your trials. I also want you to remember that God knows what you're dealing with and that He hasn't forgotten about you.

One of the greatest testaments that God doesn't forget us during our storm is Genesis 8:1, "But God remembered Noah and all the animals and all the livestock that were with him in the ark; and God caused a wind to pass over the earth, and the water subsided." God remembered Noah, and He remembers us as we deal with our tribulations.

Noah, his wife, sons, daughters-in-law, and representatives of every living creature were in the ark approximately one hundred and fifty days before the water receded. Another six months passed before they left the ark. When they finally did leave, God had plans for Noah. He directed Noah to fill the earth. God has expectations specific to our circumstances after our storm as well. That's when the work of healing, growth, thankfulness, etc., begins.

We can view our storms as having three acts; before, during, and after. Not always, but sometimes there are warning signs or red flags before we enter our storms. God forewarned Noah of what He planned to do because the world was wicked. After the warning, Noah found himself on the ark, enduring the storm.

During the storm, Noah and his family had no knowledge of the world outside the ark. They had no idea when the doors would finally open for them to disembark. Does this sound familiar? During our storm, we have no idea when it will end. What do you think went through Noah's mind during that time? Did God talk to him during those three hundred-plus days that Noah and his family were inside the ark? Or was God silent?

When Noah and his family finally left the ark, they may have thought their storm was over. It was far from over as God assigned Noah another major task. Genesis 9:7, "As for you, be fruitful and multiply; populate the earth abundantly and multiply in it." As Christians, we should understand that once we're out of the storm, God may assign tasks that are for His purposes.

PERSONAL REFLECTION

If you're dealing with a storm or a particularly difficult life challenge, take a moment to consider where you are in your storm and pray to God for the specific help you need. Remember James 4:2, which says, "you have not because you ask not."

1. **Where are you in your storm – before, during, or after?**

2. **What, if any, warnings did you receive before your storm hit?**

3. **How did you respond to the warning you received?**

4. **Have you heard from God in the midst of your storm?**

5. **What next steps do you think God will assign you?**

CHAPTER 2

Ask and Receive

"Therefore, the Lord will give you meat and you shall eat. You shall eat, not one day, nor two days, nor five days, nor ten days, nor twenty days, but a whole month, until it comes out of your nostrils and becomes loathsome to you."

. . .

NUMBERS 11:18-20

A s the police officer drove to what I presumed was the county jail, I scooched along the backseat, trying to get comfortable. My hands were cuffed behind my back, and without using them, I couldn't get ahold of the hard plastic seat. Unfortunately, I worsened my position and landed awkwardly on my right elbow. Disappointed that I was sitting in a worse position than that I had started, I gave up, sighed, and stared out the window. I hung my head in shame and mumbled, "Did I really just get arrested?" I fought back tears as I watched the trees, houses, and buildings go by. I shook my head in disbelief and thought of my parents. They had taught me the importance of responsibility, good character, and self-sufficiency. I heard my father in my mind saying, "At the end of the day, you can only depend on yourself." I leaned my head on the window and replayed the details that led to me sitting in the back of a police car.

Jerry didn't have the emotional capacity to concern himself with my feelings or well-being. To mask his pain, he prioritized another woman and getting drunk with his new friends; he no longer included me in how he spent his time or the decisions he made.

We went from sharing our whereabouts, to him strolling out of the house without as much as a goodbye. He rarely shared where he was going or when he would return. The blatant disregard for the common courtesy of sharing normal daily details hurt like a slap in the face. I became angry at his emotional neglect.

At first, he used our arguments as an excuse to drink. Then, drinking became a habit. When he wasn't drinking at home, he would go to a local dive bar. I felt helpless in my pursuit to persuade him to stop drinking. My concern for his excessive drinking remained top of mind, but I soon noticed another change in his behavior that concerned me even more than his drinking.

I can't recall the exact instance or moment, when I noticed a change in our intimacy over time. Our sweetness was gone. We weren't holding hands, pecking each other on the cheek, or cuddling. I missed the simplicity of holding hands and couch cuddles. Everything between us was off. The lack of sweetness towards one another hurt. Eventually, Jerry stopped initiating sex and rejected me when I tried. I knew his sexual appetite, and I couldn't help but think that if he wasn't having sex with me, he must be having it with someone else.

Early in our marriage, we rarely went several days without having sex. At this point in the marriage, our sexless days turned to weeks and then months. I questioned him, "Why aren't we having sex?" "Who are you having sex with – because you're not having it with me?" "What is going on?"

Jerry adamantly denied having an affair. He repeatedly told me that I had manufactured an affair in my mind, and that I was crazy. Yet, the signs were there. I knew he was having an affair, which was gut-wrenching enough, but the denials and blatant lies cut like a knife. Each subsequent lie felt like I was repeatedly being stabbed. Even though my pain was emotional, I envisioned physical cuts on my body. My pain ran deep as I dealt with his dishonesty.

I kept thinking, *Why can't he be honest with me his wife, his best friend?* I asked for the millionth time, "Jerry, what is going on?" I continued, "I get it. Marriage is hard. Just talk to me."

Emotionlessly, he responded, "I love you, Tika. I want our marriage." Hearing those words sent me into hysterics because they were the opposite of his actions. I couldn't comprehend how he could "love" me and treat me like he did. I demanded that he leave to be with his mistress. With an air of pseudo-chivalry, he retorted that he'd never leave his family. It enraged me each time he said those words. Like a child, I stomped my feet and screamed at the top of my lungs, demanding that he stop lying to me!

My accusations and his denials led to shouting matches and shoving bouts. Amid our fights, we destroyed many of our household belongings. The fights began to escalate, and for our safety, I turned his gun over to the police. Relieved that neither of us had access to the gun any longer, I still felt a tinge of guilt that I took the gun without his knowledge. So I provided him with the detective's name and number and the details of how to retrieve his weapon if he wanted to get it back. To my knowledge, he never contacted the detective. Our arguments and fights continued as if on a loop. I'd accuse him of infidelity, he'd angrily deny it, and we'd fight. I wish we would have known and understood Psalm 37:8, "Cease from anger and abandon wrath; do not get upset; it leads only to evildoing." Had we known this passage, I believe we would've handled our issues differently.

All I wanted was for Jerry to admit his infidelity. Not receiving his admission wreaked havoc on my body. I lost sleep. I craved unhealthy greasy foods. Beside myself with anxiety, I obsessed about how to uncover the truth. I wondered, should I hire a private investigator, or did I have the temerity to follow him myself? I was losing my mind.

I even went as far as to search Google for answers. During one of my searches, I stumbled upon a site for spyware and surveillance tools. It piqued my interest, and I continued to scope out the website. Even though I wanted answers, the thought of spying on him left me with a bad feeling. I didn't want to be deceitful. Then, one day out of the blue, he went off the grid for the entire day without answering my calls or responding to my text messages. His radio silence was the final straw. Depressed, angry, and demoralized, I decided to take matters into my own hands.

I accessed that tracker website faster than the speed of light, ordered a GPS tracker, and had it shipped to my parents' house. Less than a week after, my mother called and told me that a package had arrived for me. I quickly told her it was a Christmas gift for Jerry. It felt awful not being truthful with her. I had yelled at Jerry for lying to me, but now, I was lying. I didn't recognize it then, but in trying to prove Jerry's infidelity, I had become the type of person I despised the most - a liar and a deceiver.

Looking back, that would have been the time to seek assistance from my parents. Yet in my desperate state of mind, I didn't want to share my plans with them. They would've talked me out of spying on Jerry if I had. Desperate for answers about Jerry's affair, I chose to keep my plans to myself. I now know that living in secrecy is often a gateway for sinful actions. Isaiah 29:15 says, "Woe to those who deeply hide their plans from the Lord, and whose deeds are done in a dark place, and they say, who sees us? Or who knows us?" I hid my plans, thinking no one would learn of my actions.

Once at my parents, I sat and visited with them before taking the package and driving to a strip mall parking lot just a few blocks from their house. I parked away from the other cars. I sat in my car as heat surged throughout my body and sweat pooled on my upper lip and nose. I leaned out the door, expecting to vomit. Deep down, I knew my actions were wrong.

I calmed down but damaged the box in my haste to open it. I pulled out a small gray tracker, half the size of an old-school beeper. The website advertised it to parents as small enough to go undetected in a child's backpack. I remembered that Jerry had a backpack he carried every day. I mulled over the possibility of hiding it there, but if he found it, there would be an all-out war between us. I decided hiding the tracker somewhere in his truck would be better. It arrived with a fully charged battery. All I had to do was hide it.

The same night that I picked up the tracker from my parent's house, I waited for Jerry to fall asleep, and then like a thief in the night, I carried out my crime. He always parked his truck in our driveway. We had a two-stall garage, but my Jeep and Jerry's second car were parked there, so his main truck stayed in the driveway. Opening the garage would have made too much noise. Instead, I exited the kitchen door leading to the backyard, snuck out the fence gate, and tiptoed to the front of the house where his truck was parked. The only sound to be heard came from the crickets of the night. The silence and darkness sent a shiver down my spine. I didn't like the dark, even if it was just at the front of my house, but I was desperate.

I had already searched the kitchen junk drawer for a box cutter. Jerry stored several there for when packages arrived. Once I opened the passenger door, it took me less than a minute to cut a small hole in the carpet on the passenger side floorboard. I placed the device securely in the opening, positioned the carpet back in place, and scurried back inside the house.

The following day at work, I set up my tracker account and minimized it on my computer screen. Every few minutes or so, I opened and refreshed the screen, but it continued to show no activity. It wasn't long before the tracker showed movement during one of my "account refreshes." He left the house and was on his way somewhere. My eyes widened. I recognized the streets he was driving along.

I suddenly started having heart palpitations as the tracker recorded his route. *"Was it working?" "What had I done?"* I felt nauseous about spying on him. I couldn't turn back now and wondered if I should take a screenshot and confront him later that night. But that would give me away. No, that wouldn't work. Yes, I would screenshot it and keep it until I confronted him – whenever that would be, I wasn't quite sure. I hadn't thought this through.

Then, suddenly wanting to pee, I locked my laptop and walked to the bathroom. Sitting there, the sensation went away. I sat a little longer— still nothing. I flushed, washed my hands, and returned to my desk to think things through more. Once I returned to my desk, I refreshed the tracker site again. This time it showed that he was at a home that I suspected was his mistress' house. I began to shake, and just like that, I decided to forego my original plan to take a screenshot of the app. Instead, I informed my boss and coworkers that I was nauseous and not feeling well and would be leaving for the day.

Filled with anxiety, I ran to my car once I reached the parking lot. My hands shook as I inserted the key in the ignition. Every movement was quick and hurried as I secured my seat belt and pulled onto the main street. I drove recklessly, barely made some yellow lights, and went through other clearly red lights. I wanted to get to the assumed mistress' house before Jerry left. I needed to prove to him that I knew about the affair and that I wasn't crazy like he proclaimed.

I wanted to prove his unfaithfulness, but then I would be forced into making a decision I had avoided. Would I ask for a divorce? A separation? As much as I wanted proof of his affair, I didn't know how I would respond to this revelation.

Following the directions I had plugged into my maps, I turned down the street where the woman I suspected of having an affair with Jerry lived. At first, I didn't immediately spot Jerry's truck. I passed by a few houses and drove into an industrial parking lot to turn around and search the parked cars again. Just as I prepared to exit the lot, I spotted his blue Ford F-150. There was his truck. I had found him. The tracker had worked, and I wasn't crazy! The nervousness and angst I felt leading up to that moment immediately turned to rage.

The car jerked forward as I slammed the brakes into the floorboard. I thrust the gear into park and yanked the keys out of the ignition. I pushed the car door open and jumped out. Slamming the door behind me, I marched up to her house. This was it. I would catch him with her and prove to him and myself that I was not crazy.

There wasn't a front porch or entrance, so I walked to the side of her house. There were two doors. The first door opened to a flight of stairs that appeared to lead to an upstairs apartment, and I assumed the other door led to the lower-level apartment. Confident I had the correct address, I didn't know which apartment she lived in. I ran from door to door, screaming and pounding on each one.

In hindsight, I do not doubt that by the grace of God, no one answered either of those doors, pointing a gun in my face. I had acted in secrecy, so no one knew my whereabouts. Anything could have happened to me. God protected me from injury and harm.

In a fit of rage, I continued in my wrath. "Jerry, come out! Jerry, come out!" I yelled at the top of my lungs. "I know you're here!" After yelling his name for several minutes at the top of my lungs, someone finally opened the door from the lower unit, and I stood face-to-face with the woman I assumed was having an affair with my husband. She yelled, "He's not here!" Her admission confirmed that I had the right house and person, and the next thing I knew, I hit her several times in the face. Everything happened so fast, almost like I had blacked out. Mentally, I wasn't in a good place when I arrived there, and after seeing her, I paced like a lioness preparing to pounce on my prey.

I screamed and yelled for Jerry to come out, and the woman standing before me threatened to call the police. I struck her again and continued to scream for Jerry to show his face. "Jerry, I know you're in there!" He never stopped her from calling the police on me, his wife. Instead, he chose to stay hidden. Wow. The man I married, who promised to care for me, decided to protect himself instead. Whether intentional or not, they teamed up together to continue their deception. Meanwhile, I stood alone, thinking of my father's words, "At the end of the day, you can only depend on yourself." I wanted proof of the affair no matter the cost, and on that day, I received evidence in the worse way imaginable.

The saying "got their just desserts" comes to mind when I reflect on my actions. It means someone reaped what they sowed. The book of Numbers details this with the people of Israel. After being freed from Egypt, they complained that they no longer had choice meats to eat. Tired of their complaints, God gave them so much meat that it was coming out of their nostrils! Numbers 11:18-20 reads, "Therefore the Lord will give you meat and you shall eat. You shall eat, not one day, nor two days, nor five days, nor ten days, nor twenty days, but a whole month, until it comes out of your nostrils and becomes loathsome to you." I demanded the truth, and when I finally received it, it was as painful as consuming so much meat that it was coming out of my nostrils. Like the Israelites, I should have been more careful about my wish.

I was raised with a moral compass of hard work, adherence to rules, and self-sufficiency; my father's words, "At the end of the day, you can only depend on yourself," stung as I sat in the back of that police car.

The officer pulled into the garage of the police station and parked near a large door. He exited the car, walked to the passenger side back door, and grabbed my elbow to assist me out of the vehicle. My heart sank to the bottom of my stomach. Still holding onto my elbow, he walked me towards the large door and we entered a small room where another officer who processed me stood behind a glass partition. My mouth watered, and my stomach soured. I wanted to throw up. This was really happening.

Another officer led me to a small room with cubby compartments and lockers, where she instructed me to change out of my clothes and into a jail uniform. I thought, *Wait, you mean I'm staying?* I held back tears as she walked me towards a large glass cell. As I neared the cell, I noticed six to eight women pointing in my direction. The officer ushered me inside and I walked towards an open bench. Before I had a chance to sit, they laughed and said that I didn't look like I belonged in jail and how I looked like a teacher. They continued to laugh and asked in unison, "Lady, lady, what did you do?" I mumbled, "Matters of the heart."

I was terrified and ashamed, and sleep eluded me that night. I'm not sure how anyone can sleep in jail. I stared out the window all night and waited for the sun to come up. Broken, I revisited the events that led me to a jail cell. Full of disappointment and disgust in myself, I wanted to cry, but the tears never came.

Thankfully, I only had to spend one night in jail. My brother bailed me out the next day. When I called him from jail the night before, I asked him not to tell our parents. Unfortunately, Grand Rapids is a small town; someone recognized me and alerted my family that I had been arrested. As we drove away from the county jail, my brother informed me that my parents were waiting to see me. I slumped down in the car. I had hoped my parents would never find out. I didn't want to see them right away, so I told him to take me home so I could shower and I would drive myself to their house later that night.

I felt sick on the drive to their house, and when I parked out front, my emotions overcame me. I felt incredibly sad and downright low. My body ached from emotional pain as I walked to their front door. I opened the door and walked into the house, where I saw my parents sitting at the kitchen table. Even from a short distance, I saw the bewilderment on their faces. Depending on the moment when they found out, I imagine they replayed different scenarios in their minds. *Tika wouldn't steal – she has a good job. She's a kind person, and she wouldn't injure or murder anyone.* I know that they were at a complete loss.

Like many families, my parent's kitchen table was the epicenter of our family life. Sitting down at the table, I was flooded with memories of everything I had learned at that kitchen table. My moral compass was defined there. I learned about being an honest and a productive member of society. We discussed everything from recent news stories to what happened at school, and to who was running for president. My parents offered sage advice and warnings. They painted the picture of the life they wanted for my brothers and me. We were to finish high school, attend college, get a good job, marry, and have a family. To live the American dream.

Overcome with sadness and hopelessness—a lump formed in my throat as I prepared my mind to confess and discuss what led me to my current situation. I inherently knew this would be the hardest conversation I'd ever had in my life.

My mind was on overdrive, and just seeing them sitting there broke my heart. I slumped down at the table, so ashamed and embarrassed that I couldn't make eye contact with either of them. Broken, I sobbed uncontrollably as I sought their forgiveness. "I'm sorry I disappointed you." In a quiet and calm voice, my father replied, "You don't have to apologize. We know you've been going through a lot. We want to know what happened."

Due to my actions, my secret had become public knowledge. Left with no choice, I finally had to admit that my marriage was not going well. Pushing past embarrassment, I shared almost everything with them. Jerry's drinking, his affair, and losing his job. My anger and depression. The truth about closing the adoption file. When I got to the point about buying the tracker to check Jerry's activity and whereabouts, my father replied, "You should've known that would have caused problems. Why didn't you seek advice from anyone?" I held my head lower and admitted I didn't want anyone to talk me out of tracking Jerry. I apologized again.

They didn't judge me. Instead, they showed me compassion and acknowledged my pain. They were the loving and supportive parents I'd always known them to be. Before I left, they made me promise to come to them before doing anything so reckless again. I promised.

I thought that my night in jail was my lowest point. But a month later, another tragedy turned my whole world upside down. My heart shattered instantly, and I was left trying to pick up the pieces.

LIFE APPLICATION
Chapter Discussion Questions

1. It hurt when I faced the reality of my father's words, "You can only depend on yourself." **What experiences have you had when you learned you could no longer depend on a loved one? When your loved ones were no longer dependable, how did you lean on God?**

2. I can't recall the exact instance or moment, but I noticed a change in our intimacy over time. Our sweetness was gone. We weren't holding hands, pecking each other on the cheek, or cuddling. I missed the simplicity of holding hands and couch cuddles. Over time, relationships and friendships can change. **When have you experienced a relationship that you valued changed for the worse? It can be a friend, co-worker, family member, or spouse. How did you try to repair the friendship?**

3. The tracker had worked, and I wasn't crazy! The nervousness and angst I felt leading up to that moment immediately turned to rage. Read Ephesians 4:26. **What are some ways to manage our anger so we don't sin?**

4. I demanded the truth, and when I finally received it, it was just as painful as consuming so much meat that it was coming out of my nostrils. Like the Israelites, I should have been more careful about my wish. **When have you wanted something so desperately that you didn't wait for God?**

5. My parent's kitchen table was the epicenter of our family life. My moral compass was defined there. I was taught about being an honest productive member of society. **Where or how was your moral compass defined?**

BIBLE STORY

I don't have to tell you how challenging it is to wait, especially when waiting for your life to change, for healing, or for the hurt to stop. Perhaps, as you read "Ask and Receive," you wondered – if God knows your anguish, then what is taking Him so long to resolve it for you? Perhaps you even had moments of wanting to take matters into your own hands.

Before you strike out on your own, I want to share a cautionary tale with you. Take Saul, for example. He was impatient and took matters into his own hands. As a result, he lost his kingdom, sanity, and life. 1 Samuel 13:12, "I thought, now the Philistines will come down against me at Gilgal, and I have not asked the favor of the Lord. So I worked up the courage and offered the burnt offering." Samuel had already informed Saul of God's plan and how God would protect him from the Philistines, but he was impatient and "worked up the courage" to do it himself. After Saul acted on his own, Samuel shared God's frustration. 1 Samuel 13:14, "But now your kingdom shall not endure. The Lord has sought for Himself a man after His own heart."

The rest of Saul's life was marred with a burning hate for David. His days were filled with schemes to kill David. He was angry that God chose another, but it was all due to his own doing. Saul refused to accept the consequences of his actions. My days were filled with anger like Saul's. Deep down, I knew Jerry had been unfaithful. I only had to wait.

When you have time, I recommend reading First Samuel. It chronicles how Saul continued to go down a dark path of spiritual destruction, all from his own doing of not waiting on and trusting God. In Saul's story, Samuel shared that God promised to act on his behalf.

We don't have a Samuel to interpret God's decisions. Yet, God responds to all of our prayers. Have you heard the saying, "God answers all prayers with either yes, no, or not now"? The challenge is being able to distinguish which answer God is giving during your season of waiting. There are many reasons why this may be the case, but most likely, what we're seeking doesn't align with God's will for our life and may not be in our best interest. God may be protecting us from ourselves. Knowing that God saves us from ourselves if we are patient is a blessing.

PERSONAL REFLECTION

If you've been fervently praying for God to intervene and you wonder if God heard your prayer, take a moment to consider the reasons behind God's no, yes, and not now answers. Pray to God for the specific help you need while you wait. Remember James 4:2, "You have not because you ask not."

1. **What is the reason behind God's "No"?**

2. **What lesson can you learn from God's "Not now"?**

3. **Why do you think God said "Yes"?**

4. **How might God be protecting you from yourself?**

5. **What are the consequences of taking matters into your own hands?**

—

CHAPTER 3

Unexpected Grief

"So Rachel died and was buried on
the way to Ephrath that is Bethlehem"

. . .

GENESIS 35:19

After Jerry and I left the movies, we stopped at a store near our house. I sat in the car and checked my phone while he went inside. There was a higher-than-normal number of missed calls and voice messages. I listened to one of many voice messages from my father.

I ran into the convenience store screaming, "Mama is dead!" Jerry was standing at the checkout counter. He had been purchasing snacks for our evening at home. Unable to move, I doubled over, grabbed at my stomach, and shouted again, "Mama is dead!" An older lady with a short afro turned and extended her arms in my direction, "Baby, baby, are you all right?" I wasn't. I shook my head in her direction. My face was drenched with tears as I continued to scream. Jerry looked bewildered as my words began to register. Mouth agape, he stood a few moments longer at the counter, staring at me. Then, he left the bag of snacks, grabbed me around the waist, and led me to the door.

I followed him as he whispered, "Shhh, calm down. Let's go." He opened the store door with his right hand while his left arm was wrapped around my waist. The older lady followed us out and asked if he needed help with me. Jerry mumbled, "Thanks, I got her," as he opened the passenger side door to his truck and helped me inside. He asked if he needed to go to the hospital or to my parent's house. In between sobs, I cried, "To mama's house."

I couldn't catch a break or my breath. Six weeks before my mother died, I was arrested for assaulting my husband's mistress. For those six weeks, my days had been filled with meetings with my lawyer. The prosecutor wanted to charge me with unlawful entry and aggravated assault. I refused to accept that charge because it was not accurate. For one, I never entered the house, and secondly, the aggravated assault charge did not reflect what happened that day.

I was terrified that my livelihood was now at the mercy of some prosecutor who didn't know me. I stressed to my lawyer that I had never been in trouble before this incident. I asked him to plead my case as an upstanding citizen who had a lapse of judgment. I had been in complete turmoil over all the back-and-forth, and I wanted to just have it behind me finally. I couldn't understand why they were so focused on taking her word over mine. His job was to fight for me.

I advocated for myself the best I could. I suggested writing a letting to the prosecutor to introduce myself and explain how I had a college degree and had been gainfully employed for well over twenty years. My lawyer assured me he would share those details on my behalf. On a couple of occasions, I tried to engage Jerry, but he refused to discuss my pending case with me. I assumed it forced him to address his guilt in the matter, so he avoided the topic. If the prosecutor and my lawyer couldn't reach an agreement that wasn't aggravated assault, I would be at risk of losing my job and reputation. If that happened, how would I provide for myself? Mentally, I was exhausted from the whole ordeal.

Stressed and unable to sleep, I called off work three days in a row. Up until this point, I prided myself on showing up and being present at work. I never let on that anything troubled me. This ordeal exhausted me so much that I didn't have the energy required to engage at work. I certainly didn't want to smile and pretend that everything was fine with my life. I desperately needed a break, so I stayed in bed for those three days. I hardly slept, though, as I constantly had "what if" thoughts about my case. After the third straight day, Jerry walked into the bedroom and asked if I wanted to go to a movie. Figuring it might be a good idea to leave my bed, I agreed to go. I thought any opportunity to spend time with him could repair our marriage.

Before we left for the movie, I called my mother. I talked to her every day, even if it was just a few minutes. I heard the excitement in her voice when she answered. My niece and great-niece, who was only a month old at the time, were at her house. My mom exclaimed, "I have big company visiting me! I'll call you back later." I replied, "Have fun, and I'll talk to you when I leave the movies." Little did I know that would be the last time I spoke to my mother.

After leaving the convenience store, I cried the entire drive to my parents' house. When we arrived, all the parking spaces were occupied, so Jerry told me to go ahead inside, and he would find a spot down the street. I immediately jumped out of the truck and ran onto the front porch, where several family members were standing with sullen looks on their faces. Someone opened the screen door and helped me inside. Once inside, I found the house full of people all standing around, crying and hugging each other. I scanned their faces as I quickened my steps to reach the dining room.

There, I found my mother. Sprawled out on the dining room floor. I collapsed on top of her and wailed uncontrollably. *How could this be?* I had just talked to her a few hours before when she sounded so strong and joyful, and now here she was, dead on the floor. I continued to embrace her for quite some time, and I'm not sure if I got up on my own or if someone picked me up. All I remember is that my father eventually asked me to go upstairs to their bedroom to get my mother's address book. He had to make additional phone calls to inform more family and friends.

After I retrieved the address book, I walked back downstairs and noticed that my husband had made his way into the house in the sea of grieving people. I spotted him sitting in a corner of the kitchen, alone. Instead of comforting and grieving alongside my family, whom he'd known since he was fifteen years old, he fixated on his phone. My mother had just died, yet I felt dread and anxiety over the thought of him texting his mistress. Just like that, Jerry's affair consumed my thoughts yet again. I glared at him. He looked up, and we made brief eye contact with each other.

Normally, I would've asked him whom he was texting, but instead, I continued to glare at him. He finally broke the silence and asked if I was okay. I nodded, sighed, and walked back to the dining room. I sat and waited for the funeral home to arrive to retrieve my mother's body. It felt like an eternity, even though only fifteen minutes had elapsed. The entire time I waited for the funeral home, I worried about who or what kept Jerry's attention on his phone. He never joined me in the dining room to wait with me or comfort me.

I never properly grieved my mother because every thought I had focused on Jerry. When I pictured my mother's dead body, my mind immediately thought of him sitting in the corner alone with his phone, texting. My marital problems overshadowed my mother's death, and it made me sick to my stomach. Jerry never left my thoughts, yet he didn't deserve for me to be thinking so much about him, especially at this time. When my mind wasn't fixated on Jerry, I thought about my court case.

My legal troubles kept me up at night. I feared losing my job and income because I had no idea what my legal issues meant. Whenever I sat alone, my mind would go to my mother, but within minutes drifted to the chaos that had become my life. This chaos affected my ability to grieve my mother how I thought she should be mourned.

My mother and I had a loving, supportive, and fun relationship. As the only girl out of four children, my mother and I had a close and special bond. We talked every day and several times throughout the day. I remember my father once asked what we could possibly talk about several times a day. Laughing, I told him, "Everything."

We discussed and planned family trips that Jerry and I went on with her and my father. Our conversations ranged from news of the day to shopping and cooking. She had an amazing smothered steak and mashed potatoes recipe that Jerry loved. He requested it every year for his birthday, and she happily made it just for him. It was his favorite meal, and once I thought I'd give it a try and surprise him. It was an absolute disaster. I shared my effort with my mother, and she teased me relentlessly. We had many laughs about that disastrous meal I prepared for Jerry. A day didn't go by that we didn't enjoy being in each other's company. She was truly my best friend.

Yes, she deserved reverence from her only daughter, for me to be inconsolable, to barely be able to climb out of bed after her passing. As I replayed in my mind how I wanted to mourn her, I couldn't help but think of the short mention of Rachel's death in the Bible. Genesis 35:19, "So Rachel died and was buried on the way to Ephrath that is Bethlehem." There was no mention of the Israelites putting on ashes or wearing sackcloth – just the one sentence that she died and was buried. The reality is that our loved ones die, and we bury them.

It took some time for me to accept that I didn't have to wail and be inconsolable after losing my mother. Ecclesiastes 12:7, tells us, "Then the dust will return to the earth as it was, and the spirit will return to God who gave it." In time, I learned to be at peace knowing my mother's spirit returned to God.

In truth, my mother would have wanted me to take care of business and get on with life. My parents didn't coddle me. Even through my fog of grief, I could hear her quipping, "Girl, get it together. You don't have time to be moping around."

So I did what she would have expected of me and got to work. My sister-in-law, niece, and I began to make preparations. I periodically asked my dad and brothers for input, and they responded that they trusted our judgment. So I pushed forward. During the day, I visited with family and friends who delivered food and flowers to my parents' house. I made phone calls and ran errands to plan my mother's funeral. At night, I crawled into bed and cried about my court case and marriage. Running on fumes, I desperately wanted to retreat to my bed and stay there.

I also wanted to be comforted by Jerry and to comfort him. I know her death hurt him, as well. He'd known my mother since he was fifteen years old, and they loved one another. I'd like to think that we offered some form of reciprocal comfort, but for the life of me, I can't remember. Unfortunately, my mind resorted to our marital drama, pain, and agony. It breaks my heart that I can't remember how we supported one another after my mother's death.

I do recall once when I tried to comfort Jerry after his grandmother's death. Frustrated at my words, he yelled, "Your mother is still here! You don't understand." At the time, I thought he despised me because my mother was still alive. Now my mother was dead, and the pain was unbearable. I finally understood the excruciating pain Jerry held in his heart after losing his mother and grandmother. I felt lost and empty. I had no idea how I would navigate life without my mother.

On the day of the funeral, we took a family picture while we waited for the limo to arrive. I don't remember much after that. I can't recall the color of the dress we purchased for her to wear or even the color of her casket. I don't know what verse the pastor referenced for the eulogy or which songs were played. With the stress I was experiencing from my marriage and my mother dying, it's no wonder my memory bank was empty. However, the memories I couldn't recall were replaced with fond memories of our life together.

After burying my mother, my father sat my brothers and me down and said that he and my mother promised each other that whoever was left would keep the family together. They knew of families who struggled to maintain relationships after a loved one died, and they promised not to allow that to happen to our family. He stressed how he wanted us to remain close and support one another. He encouraged us to start a new tradition: meeting every Saturday for breakfast. These weekly breakfasts together allowed us to check in on one another and have quality time together.

One Saturday, my brothers and I were emotional as we lamented how much we missed our mom. My father said he missed her, too, and then he reminded us how blessed we were to have had her. My father never stopped teaching us how to navigate life. I'm reminded of Proverbs 1:8, "Hear, my son, your father's instruction and do not forsake your mother's teaching." He offered instruction on how to manage our sadness by reminiscing about the good times. He recounted how they met. His face radiated joy as he smiled and laughed and shared how my mother had turned him down three times before she agreed to go on a date with him.

Still smiling, he commented that God had put them together. His treks down memory lane encouraged us to do the same. By not focusing on or having memories of when she died, I celebrated my mother's wonderful life. My dad encouraged us to honor her memories, so we published memorandums on the anniversary of my mother's death in the newspaper. We visited her grave on Memorial Day and thanked God for gifting my mother to our family.

Following his lead to focus on happier times, I started to challenge myself to recreate some of her recipes. I visualized how she moved about her kitchen and prepared meals. Right now, my attempts are still a work in progress! I'm confident that the day will come when I master a couple of her recipes. Through my father's godly support and teaching, I stopped blaming myself for not grieving. I began to move towards a semblance of healing. I hadn't healed completely, but I was certainly in a better place.

Unfortunately, the better place I found myself in didn't last long. Four months after burying my mother, my marriage to Jerry finally reached its breaking point, and I was forced to make a decision that completely changed my life.

LIFE APPLICATION

Chapter Discussion Questions

1. I wanted to grieve my mother. She deserved reverence from her only daughter, for me to be inconsolable, and to barely be able to climb out of bed. At least, that's how I felt I should have responded to her passing. Everyone grieves differently. **When have you struggled to grieve a loved one the way you believed you should have?**

2. My dad encouraged us to start a new tradition. As a family, we started meeting every Saturday for breakfast. It allowed us to check in on one another and have quality time together. **Why is it important to maintain or start new family traditions after losing a beloved family member?**

3. My dad encouraged us to honor my mother's memories. **How does honoring the memories of family members help with the grieving process?**

4. On the day of the funeral, we took a family picture while we waited for the limo to arrive. I don't remember much after that. **When have you experienced a loss where you struggled to remember details of the death or funeral? What circumstances do you think impacted your memory?**

5. By not focusing on or having memories of when she died, I was able to celebrate my mother's wonderful life. **How do you celebrate the lives of your loved ones?**

BIBLE STORY

The drama of my life distracted me from grieving my mother's death in the way I thought I should have grieved her. I obsessed over my lack of grieving. Unbeknownst to me, God was stirring up my life to prepare me to trust and depend on Him. A verse that resonates with me is Deuteronomy 32:11, "Like an eagle that stirs up its nest, that hovers over its young, He spread His wings and caught them, He carried them on His pinions." I love listening to pastors teach on this verse. Many will use this to illustrate how our Heavenly Father cares for us, much like an eagle cares for its young.

Parents care for us, teach us to depend on them, and prepare us for the next phase in life. The eagle stirs up its nest to awaken the eaglets out of the familiarity of their present situation. To be awakened from their familiarity is needed to prepare the eaglets to eventually take flight. The mother eagle rips the warm, soft woolly layer to reveal the thorns and other prickly materials underneath. The composition or familiarity of the nest is no longer comfortable, so the eaglets climb to the edge to avoid the exposed prickly sticks.

Perched on the edge and unaware of their new surroundings, the eaglets take a step and clumsily fall out of the nest. The father eagle is nearby, watching the activities unfold. Just as the eaglets fall, he quickly spreads his wings, swoops them up, and carries them back to the safety of the nest. The father continues to swoop in and carry them on his pinions until they learn to fly independently. Soon, they'll leave the nest, confident, secure, and ready to prepare the next generation of eaglets to take flight.

Reading this brief story, can you imagine how God cares for us, much like the eagle cares for its young? For His purposes, God stirs up the familiarity of our lives. Sometimes, we need to be forced out of what is familiar, especially if it keeps us from God. Like the eagle, we may find ourselves on the edge of life, where we fall and stumble. God, never far from us, swoops in and carries us to safety. Our safety lies in Him.

We continue to fall, and He swoops in to save us no matter how many times we fall. Soon, we learn to remain in the safety of God. Now, secure and confident, we are ready to completely have faith in and trust God no matter what life may throw our way. I believe God prepared my earthly father to teach me how our Heavenly Father is an eagle and swoops in to carry me back to safety. As mentioned in my story, I shared how my brothers and I lamented at breakfast. We were on the edge of life – despondent and certainly prey to enter into destructive grieving behaviors. Just as we began to feel hopeless, my earthly father swooped in and carried us safely to the warm and loving memories of our home and our mother.

Just like the eaglets, we went down that despondent path a second, third, and fourth time and each time, my father was always nearby, ready to encourage us. Today, my brothers and I have taken on the responsibility of the father eagle, and we encourage one another just as my father did.

The drama of my marriage, being arrested, and losing my mother all upended my life in ways I hadn't anticipated. Yet, through stirring up my life, God taught me to find safety in Him.

PERSONAL REFLECTION

Are you in a familiar situation that perhaps God may need to stir up? Take a moment to consider how God is stirring up your life to bring you to His safety. Pray to God for the specific help you need. Remember James 4:2, "You have not because you ask not."

1. **How has God stirred up your life?**

2. **What familiar situation do you need to step away from?**

3. When have you fallen and stumbled?

4. When has God carried you back to safety?

5. What does safety in God mean to you?

CHAPTER 4

The End of an Era

"But I want you to be free from concern.
One who is unmarried is concerned about
things of the Lord, how he may please the Lord"

. . .

1 CORINTHIANS 7:32

I arrived home from work, pulled into the driveway, and parked my car in the garage. I exited the car, grabbed my lunch bag and purse, and walked to the mailbox at the end of the driveway. I opened it, reached in, and grabbed the mail. Out of habit, I sorted through the mail as I walked back towards the house. I noticed a letter with the return address of the judge assigned to my divorce. *That's strange*, I thought. My divorce hearing had been two months ago; what could this letter from the judge mean? Full of angst and uncertainty, I worried I might have to return to court. Jerry contested the first hearing by mailing me a certified notice. I wanted this to be over and dreaded being summoned to attend the hearing Jerry requested.

After a few more moments, I decided to deal with whatever the letter contained. I ripped it open. It was the divorce decree. I quickly scanned the details. Everything looked correct: plaintiff, defendant, addresses, etc. Then my eyes drifted to the judge's official stamp towards the bottom of the page. I took a deep breath when I realized I actually held the official dissolution of my marriage in my hands. I trembled. I shook my head and sighed in disbelief. Our nineteen-year marriage had come to an end.

Standing in the driveway, holding my official divorce, I replayed the events that led to my filing for divorce. I had finally sought help to leave

Jerry on the night of my release from jail. When I arrived home that night, I pulled into the garage and entered the kitchen through the side door. My dogs greeted me with wagging tails. Like an assembly line, I scratched each one behind their ears and petted their bodies. They followed me as I somberly walked through the house. I touched furniture and stared at family pictures. I leaned on doorframes and recalled memories we had shared in each room. I didn't know what would become of being arrested, but I worried I could potentially lose my livelihood and everything I valued in my home. I had never felt so low in my life.

When I reached the bedroom, I removed my clothes and dumped them near the closet door. I didn't have the energy to put them away properly. I grabbed a t-shirt from the dresser, threw myself on the bed, and wailed like a banshee. I thrashed around, screaming and crying. Drenched with sweat and tears, I gasped for breath. There was no doubt I was in the throes of a full-on panic attack. I've never had a panic attack before, and it frightened me.

Instinctively, I placed my hand over my heart, in my mind protecting it from a panic attack. I managed to slow my breathing down. My breath eventually felt normal, but my hands trembled as I wiped the tears from my face. Still holding my heart, I felt calmer. I sat up, stared across the bedroom, and pleaded out loud, "God, if he is ever with her again, please give me the strength to leave him." Without as much as an Amen, I moved my hands along the bed and found a spot that wasn't wet with sweat and tears. I curled into a ball and shut my eyes. I didn't remember falling asleep when I woke up the next morning. I instinctively checked my phone to see if Jerry had contacted me. He hadn't come home after I had been released from jail, and I wondered if he had tried to call me. There weren't any messages or missed phone calls from him. It hurt that he didn't call to check on me.

As much as I wanted to believe otherwise, when I prayed out loud to God, I had come to terms with the fact that my marriage was over. Jerry had been living a life that no longer included me. Broken, I had become the other woman who begged for his time and attention. I still cared for and loved my husband, but his actions made it apparent that Jerry no longer cared for me in the same manner.

Getting arrested left me exhausted, dejected, and depressed. I was at the absolute lowest point in my life and I felt that I had no choice but to turn to God for strength to do what I couldn't do on my own, to leave Jerry. I tried everything I thought would save my marriage. I offered myself sexually. I suggested counseling, to which he begrudgingly agreed to attend one session only to storm out in an aggressive rage. He vowed never to return because he felt the counselor was on my side. I reached out to his best friend for help and advice. I begged him to talk to me and to help me understand what I could do differently. I took steps that I hoped would repair my marriage and blamed myself when it never improved. Despite trying all of those things, and many more, I never asked God to intervene to heal our hearts and restore our marriage.

Even during our "Job trials" that I shared about in chapter one, I never prayed for my husband, myself, or our marriage. I can't help but wonder how God would have moved in our marriage had I prayed. I'm ashamed to admit it, but I put all of my faith in Jerry and myself. In the past, when we'd had marital issues, we were able to sit down and work through them. I honestly believed that we could fix everything on our own, just like we had in the past. We didn't have the wherewithal to pray then, so it never occurred to me to do it when we were in turmoil. Sadly, we didn't know Psalm 118:8, "It is better to take refuge in the Lord than to trust in people." I believe I would have sought God if I'd had this knowledge.

Have you heard the saying, "God has a way of humbling you"? It's not just a saying; it's true. When I went to jail and had to confess my secrets and sins to my parents, it humbled me in ways I never imagined. I had to admit the hard truth that my anger controlled me and landed me in jail. My rage was out of control. If I didn't control that burning fire within myself, I would continue to self-destruct. I could no longer blame Jerry; I had to deal with my own problem. I needed help. I needed God. Psalm 55:22, "Cast your burden upon the Lord, and He will sustain you." Broken, I used God as a last resort, yet He was gracious to me. He heard and answered my prayer.

Four months passed after my desperate, last resort prayer to God. Those months were far from perfect, but we had experienced some decent days. Things were still strained, but it seemed that we didn't argue as much. I think we were both tired of the fights. I know I was certainly tired of fighting. We did just enough to get along. There were no real efforts to restore the marriage to what it had once been. We were just going through the motions.

Then one day, on my way home from work, I called Jerry. I heard the moodiness in his voice. He started a fight with me. This happened whenever he wanted an excuse to leave home for any amount of time he felt he needed to "calm down." I rolled my eyes, and much to my own disappointment, I engaged in the argument. He ended the call like he always did when we argued by shouting, "Phone off!" And just like that, he shut off all forms of communication with me.

I shrugged my shoulders and tossed my cell phone onto the passenger seat. I drove home in silence. When I pulled into the driveway, I immediately noticed Jerry's truck wasn't there. It didn't surprise me to see that he had left already. I sighed, backed out of the driveway then drove to his mistress' house. Despite my court order to not be within five-hundred feet of her, I drove to her house anyway. As I anticipated, I saw Jerry's truck parked in the driveway of his mistress' house. Surprisingly, I stayed calm. The last time I had showed up at her house, I raged with anger. This time, instead of storming her house, I parked a few houses down from hers and just sat in my car. I took a deep breath, exhaled, shook my head, and mouthed to myself: *I can't do this anymore.* I sat staring at his truck for five minutes more, then I started my Jeep and drove home. I wasn't angry. I was done.

He was gone the entire weekend. I periodically checked my phone to see if he had contacted me. He didn't. I didn't contact him either. I went about my weekend as normal. I took care of the dogs, cleaned, and did laundry on Saturday, and on Sunday morning, I met my dad and brothers at church.

After church, my family and I agreed to meet an hour later for lunch. I drove home to freshen up and change clothes. I had just finished re-applying eyeliner when Jerry walked into the bathroom, where I stood fixing my makeup. He leaned against the doorframe, and without me saying a word, he proceeded to offer his standard lie of why he stayed away the entire weekend. I stared directly into his eyes and, with courage I didn't know I had within me, said, "Go back to wherever you spent the weekend. I'm filing for divorce." I wasn't angry. I was done.

He looked relieved, which surprised me. I expected him to rant about how I was overacting. I thought, wait a minute. Had he been waiting for me to end it? He repeatedly told me he would never leave his family. Perhaps, he wanted me to be the one to make the official call to end the marriage all along. That way, he could continue with the story that I manufactured the affair in my crazy mind. So if anyone said to him, "I can't believe you and Tika are no longer together," he could throw up his hands and claim ignorance on his part. I can't say for sure if that was his reasoning, but it certainly felt that way at the time.

After I declared to Jerry that I would be filing for divorce and told him to return to wherever he'd spent the weekend, he stared at me for what felt like ten seconds and walked out of the house. I felt stronger than I'd ever felt. I finished getting ready, then drove to the restaurant to meet my family. I arrived later than everyone else. It was a nice spring day, so they were outside, and I assumed they were waiting for our table. I noticed my brothers standing on the opposite end of the building.

They were engaged in a conversation while they smoked cigarettes. I waved to the family sitting on the bench and walked toward my brothers. Without much thought, I blurted out, "Jerry was gone all weekend; it's over. I'm filing for divorce." I think I blurted it out because I needed to convince myself. I wasn't angry. I was done.

In unison, they questioned, "What?" I shared everything that had transpired over the weekend. Like the loving and supportive brothers they are, they said, "No one will think badly of you if you want to continue to work on the marriage." I thanked them for their support but said I was done. I waited until later that afternoon when I visited my father at his house to tell him. His response didn't surprise me, "Well, it's good in a way. We love Jerry, but don't want him to continue mistreating you." He knew what I had endured and wanted me to be at peace and happy.

The very next day at work, I searched online and found a petition for divorce. Without hesitation, I completed the documents, printed copies, drove straight to the County Clerk's office on my lunch hour, and filed the paperwork. I cried the entire drive back to my job but never questioned my decision. I wasn't angry. I was done.

The sound of a car driving by brought me back to holding the letter from the judge. My hands trembled as I continued to scan the divorce decree. I felt a tinge of shame and embarrassment that I had failed to keep my marriage. I sighed as the reality hit me in ways I hadn't anticipated. *Now what.* I wasn't quite sure what I was supposed to do next. I felt lost.

Immediately my legs buckled, and tears filled my eyes. I flipped through the pages, not sure what I was looking for. The divorce decree had been signed and dated September 3, 2013. I hoped to see something, anything, that would explain why the judge signed and certified my divorce on September 3rd – which had been the same date on which we were married.

Tears impeded my vision as I continued to read. Then my eyes found the assertion I had made to return to my maiden name. The decree and approval to return to my maiden name confirmed that Jerry and I were officially divorced. I stared at my maiden name with mixed emotions. I felt dread as I thought of the work required to complete the name change, like updating my driver's license, bank account, work email, etc. Still standing in the driveway, I looked up from the letter and finally walked into the house. I remember wanting to be hugged and comforted, but there was no one.

I sat at the kitchen table and cried. My thoughts were scattered as I kept saying out loud, "Why September 3rd?" I wondered if it meant that my marriage wasn't ordained by God. But the date of the divorce decree didn't matter. I had prayed for the strength to leave him if he was ever with his mistress again, and all that mattered is that God had given me the strength I had prayed for.

It took some time, but when I sat and reflected on all the drama I had suffered through during the last few years of my marriage, I asked myself, "What was I fighting for?" Even if he had ended the affair and we worked things out, it'd only be a matter of time before the next affair. Jerry had actually had other affairs over the years, and I somehow managed to stick it out with him.

Today, I'm glad to be off the infidelity merry-go-round finally, and I'm glad my marriage didn't survive. I believe in marriage and loved Jerry, but our lives had become too tumultuous to stay together. I'm especially thankful that the marriage didn't survive because I now know my divorce is one of the catalysts of my renewed faith. Knowing that God gave me the strength to leave a marriage that was no longer good for me, I started to attend church regularly after my divorce. Still quite new in my faith, I sometimes struggled to understand the weekly sermons and how God's Word fit into my life. Then on the one-year anniversary of my mother's death, God presented Himself to me so shockingly that it changed the trajectory of my faith forever, and I had to tell others.

LIFE APPLICATION
Chapter Discussion Questions

1. I never prayed for my husband, myself, or our marriage. I'm ashamed to admit it, but I put all my faith in Jerry and myself. **How have you made prayer a priority for your spouse or significant other in your life?**

2. Read Ephesians 5:22-25, 28-29. **How might this verse change the way you pray for your spouse, yourself, and your marriage?**

3. Without much thought, I blurted out, "Jerry was gone all weekend; it's over. I'm filing for divorce." Malachi 2:16 reminds us that God hates divorce. Yet, Matthew 19:9 states specific grounds for divorce. **What are your beliefs on divorce? Is it ever warranted?**

4. I realized the problem lay with me and not Jerry. I needed help. I needed God. Psalm 55:22, "Cast your burden upon the Lord, and He will sustain you." I finally recognized that I could no longer blame my husband for my anger and actions. **Have you had an instance where you identified that the problem lay with you instead of someone else?**

5. He looked relieved, which surprised me. I expected him to rant about how I was overacting. I thought, *Wait a minute. Had he been waiting for me to end it?* **When have you realized that your husband or boyfriend was waiting on you to end the relationship?**

BIBLE STORY

If you are engaged, married, in a long-term relationship, or single, you may wonder why I admitted that I was glad my marriage ended. I want to stress that by no means am I advocating divorce. In fact, I am a firm believer and supporter of marriage. I loved being married and serving and pleasing my husband. I loved our life until it became unbearable. I never wanted my marriage to end. However, as I've had time to reflect, I believe we're not meant to be in situations that keep us from fellowship with God. Abusive relationships, adulterous marriages, and unequally yoked marriages are just a few examples of relationships that can hinder our ability to be in full fellowship with Jesus.

Today God is the head of my life. During my marriage, He was not. In fact, Jerry and I weren't prepared when confronted with the reality that God wasn't in our lives. During our marital strife, I reached out to one of Jerry's childhood friends whom he admired and respected. His friend and wife sat down opposite Jerry and me. He raised his hand to signal he was starting the conversation, then announced, "Before we get started, I want to know, is God first in your marriage?" Obviously, He wasn't. He continued, "My only advice for you is to put God first in your marriage. With Him, you'd make it; without Him, you won't." I didn't know it at the time, but his words were prophetic.

I can't help but think of Exodus 8:1, "Then the Lord said to Moses, go to Pharaoh and say to him, this is what the Lord says, let My people go, so that they may serve me." Of course, this verse refers to God's plan to liberate the Israelites from Egyptian bondage. Yet, in a way, my marriage had become a form of bondage as we were living for the world and not for God. Today, I serve and worship God. I am happiest when I'm studying and spending time with His Word. I can't say for certain if Jerry and I hadn't gotten a divorce if my relationship with God would be what it is today.

While in bondage, the Israelites couldn't worship God freely. Of course, God was certainly concerned that they were living in bondage. However, in the declarations in Exodus, God specifically used language that He wanted the Israelites freed in order to serve Him. Read Exodus 5:1, 7:16, and 9:13. In all these passages and many others in Exodus, Moses is directed to tell Pharaoh to let God's people go so they may worship Him.

From history, we know that Pharaoh considered himself a god. The Egyptians revered Pharaoh. However, God sent Moses to remind Pharaoh that He is the Lord God and to let the Israelites go to worship Him. Through the ten plagues, God repeatedly warned Pharaoh that He was the Lord God. Sometimes God has to warn us and the individuals in our lives that He is the one true God. His reminders aren't necessarily nice taps on the shoulder. Pharaoh learned the hard way. I also learned a valuable lesson when God wasn't first in my life.

PERSONAL REFLECTION

God should be the head of our lives. Yet, the reality is that sometimes we are in bondage to people, things, and places, which often interfere with our ability to serve and worship God. Take a moment to consider who or what you need to be released from so that you may serve God. Pray to God for the specific help you need. Remember James 4:2, "You have not because you ask not."

1. How do you define bondage?

2. When have you ever felt you were in bondage?

3. How do you believe that bondage interfered with your ability to worship God?

4. Are you in bondage now? If so, who or what has you bound?

5. If God is not already the center of your life, what will it mean to you to finally put Him first?

CHAPTER 5

Coming on Christian Experience

"And that from childhood you have known the sacred writings
which are able to give you the wisdom that leads to salvation
through faith which is in Christ Jesus."

. . .

2 TIMOTHY 3:15

I dreaded the thought of going to church on the anniversary of my mother's death. There were many reasons, but I didn't want to be greeted with hugs, smiles, and pecks on the cheek. I preferred to sit in my sadness as I wasn't in the mood to pretend I was fine when I wasn't, especially since I never properly grieved her when she died. I wanted to devote the day to mourning her because I knew the next day would bring another challenge I had to face.

All morning, I tried to block the images that kept flooding my mind of my mother's lifeless body sprawled out on my parent's dining room floor. I never asked how she happened to be on her back. I assumed at some point she received CPR, but I never asked anyone for some reason. Even today, I still don't know the answer to that question. I closed my eyes as thoughts from that day continued to smack me in the face like the force of a four-foot wave.

Depressed, sad, and cold, I cocooned in my comforter and settled into bed. The overcast, twenty-four-degree Michigan day rendered me unmotivated to leave my bed. I didn't want to deal with the cold or people. I shared how sad I felt and that I had decided to stay home from church with a friend over text messages. After some back and forth, I received a text that said, "Trust me. You'll feel better if you go." I rolled my eyes. I didn't want words of encouragement. I wanted to hear, "You deserve to stay in bed. Go back to sleep."

I stayed cocooned in my blankets another ten minutes or so before obligation forced me out of bed. Nowadays, I attend church because I want to, not because I feel like I have to, but, on that day, I pushed through just to get it over with.

I started the shower, attached my iPhone to the speaker, turned Pandora to shuffle, just as I always had done, and got in the shower. The first song that played was Tamela Mann's, "Take Me to the King," and the second was Yolanda Adams' "Open My Heart." I broke down and cried. Those songs made me feel seen. They offered a solution to the depression, loneliness, anger, and sadness that had become my reality. Even though those songs were the balm I needed, I was taken aback when I heard them.

I didn't have a single Gospel station in my Pandora account, but somehow these two Gospel songs played back-to-back. Was God speaking to me? It must have been divine intervention, right? What else could it be?

Prior to this, I can't ever recall an instance in my life where I felt like I received a sign from God. I'm sure there were signs, but I didn't have the spiritual maturity to recognize them. Samuel, one of the most important prophets in the Bible, also struggled to recognize God's voice early in his education. 1 Samuel 3:7-9, "Now Samuel did not yet know the Lord, nor had the word of the Lord yet been revealed to him. So, the Lord called Samuel again for the third time. And he rose and went to Eli and said, 'Here I am, for you called me.' Then Eli discerned that the Lord was calling the boy. And Eli said to Samuel, 'Go lie down, and it shall be if He calls you that you shall say, "Speak, Lord, for your servant is listening'."

It took Samuel several times to recognize that God was speaking to him. In fact, it was Eli who finally informed Samuel that it was the Lord. This interaction between Samuel and Eli resonated with me. When I heard those Gospel songs, I believed it was a sign from God. On the one-year anniversary of my mother's death, God called to me. There was no other explanation. I had to tell someone what had just happened to me.

I arrived just a few minutes before church started. My father looked at me, shook his head, and commented, "I didn't think you were going to make it. You need to go to bed earlier." I replied, "I know." I settled in next to him and prepared to listen to the sermon. If only he had known what I had just been wrestling with, he might have said something different.

During the service, the pastor asked for volunteers to come forward to testify how great God had been to them, specifically how they were blessed after graciously giving tithes to the church. Several people made their way out of the pews to give their testimonies, which always included a familiar church saying, "As tithes go up, blessings come down."

After several people shared their stories, the pastor asked if anyone else wanted to share. God had stirred something inside of me that morning, so at the last minute, I raised my hand and walked to the front of the church. Immediately, I felt everyone's eyes on me and started to regret my impulsive decision. *"There is no going back now,"* I thought as I climbed the steps to the pulpit.

I stared out at the congregation as they stared back at me. None of us knew what to expect. My stomach churned. I didn't have any prepared remarks. I wiped my sweaty hands along my skirt, took a deep breath, and started to speak.

I shared everything that had happened to me that morning. I heard shouts of "Amen!" The shouts reassured me that my words resonated. Before I knew it, I stopped talking and exhaled. Unsure of what to do next, I stood there for a few seconds staring out at the church. Then the entire congregation clapped. Their claps woke me from my temporary trance, and I stepped away from the pulpit and walked towards the steps. I eyed the steps nervously. There were only four, but I couldn't control my legs. Fearing that I might lose my footing as I descended the steps, I glanced to my right in hopes that a railing would miraculously appear. No such luck.

Slowly, I stepped down onto the first step, carefully watching my feet to ensure I didn't fall. Finally, I looked up and spied my father smiling when I reached the bottom. I concentrated on him as I walked back to the pew. As I settled in next to my dad, he exclaimed, "That was great!" I smiled a thank you to him. I wiped my upper lip as my body shivered with nervous energy. I shook my head in disbelief that I had testified in front of the entire congregation. I listened to the sound of my heartbeat until I calmed down.

Fifteen minutes or so after I testified, the order of the church service continued as normal. At the end of the service, the pastor said, "The doors of the church are open. Who here wants to have a relationship with God? Who here wants to secure their salvation with Jesus Christ?" Without a second thought, I raised my hand and walked to the front of the church. The Gospel songs that played clearly instructed me to go to God. Plus, after everything that had happened that morning, I felt a strong connection to my mother. It seemed as if she were directing me, so I walked to the front of the church, wanting to please her. I believed that God had orchestrated the events of that morning. I couldn't ignore what He stirred in me; I felt compelled to confess my faith.

The pastor, church leaders, and my father embraced me. The congregation clapped and shouted, "Amen!" Then, the pastor announced, "Tika McCoy is coming on Christian experience. She's already baptized and wants to recommit her relationship with Jesus. Join me in welcoming her to the First Community AME Church family." There were more claps and amens. I shook my head and laughed under my breath. The way my morning started, I would've never imagined confessing my faith in front of the entire congregation.

The pastor correctly announced that I had joined "on Christian experience". My family roots were deep in this church. My great-grandfather was once an assistant pastor there, and many of my extended family still attend today. I belonged to this same church many years before, where I received the sacrament of baptism. Jerry and I were also married there and attended for several years. Confessing my faith felt like going home.

My Christian experience goes back to when I was ten years old, and my grandmother picked me up to attend this same church with her, which just happened to have been on communion Sunday. I remember I couldn't wait to get home to ask my father if I really ate the body of Jesus and drank his blood! He laughed and told me I ate saltine crackers and grape juice. I thought it tasted like crackers and juice, even though the preacher said otherwise.

That was the first and last time I went to church with my grandmother. It remains one of the most important church attendances of my life. I believe my grandmother bestowed a blessing upon me that Sunday. Much like the fathers in the Old Testament who blessed their firstborn sons with inheritance, words of wisdom, and prophetic future declarations, my grandmother secured my future. By kneeling at the altar alongside her and partaking in the Lord's Supper for the first time, she ensured my covenant relationship with Jesus. My grandmother took it upon herself to start me on the right path. My grandmother's actions were obedient to Proverbs 22:6, "Train up a child in the way he should go, even when he is old he will not depart from it."

Paul, in the book of Timothy, spoke of a faithful grandmother and how she nurtured faith in her family. He praised Timothy's faithful lineage in 2 Timothy 1:5. "For I am mindful of the sincere faith within you, which first dwelt in your grandmother Lois and your mother Eunice, and I am sure that it is in you as well." Thank God for the faith of devoted grandmothers!

As my father and I walked out of the church, an older female member who usually sat in the pew directly behind my father and me approached us. "Tika, thank you for your testimony. Your testimony moved me, and I know you meant it. The other ones were asked ahead of time to encourage more tithing." Her comments shocked me. It never occurred to me that the other testimonies were preplanned "theater." I thanked her for her nice words. My father also thanked her, then turned to me, "Tik, I'm glad you joined." He often shortened my name. I smiled back at him.

While driving home from church that day, I vowed that I would focus even more on my relationship with God. Faithful to my vow, I attended church every Sunday, but for some reason, the sermons didn't speak to or draw me closer to God. I became discouraged as I really wanted to grow spiritually. I complained to my father that maybe I needed to join a different church. He commented that the church wasn't the problem. He encouraged me to read and study the Bible to increase my knowledge.

Heeding his advice, I joined the women's Bible study group, and to this day, I still regularly attend. I found pastors online who explained the Bible in a manner that helped me to understand it better. I read study Bibles that further enhanced my knowledge. The more I learned, the more my faith increased, and the more I trusted God. I can't remember exactly when it happened, but soon I was in daily fellowship with God by praying and meditating on His Word. My faith was growing, but it would be challenged yet again when my ex-husband received a terminal health diagnosis.

LIFE APPLICATION

Chapter Discussion Questions

1. I couldn't ever recall an instance in my life where I felt like I received a sign from God. I'm sure there were signs, but I didn't have the spiritual maturity to recognize them. **When have you experienced God's presence?**

2. I shook my head in disbelief that I had testified in front of the entire congregation. Many churches offer congregants the opportunity to share personal testimonies. **If given a chance, how comfortable would you be testifying in front of your church? Have you already given a testimony?**

3. And Eli said to Samuel, "Go lie down, and it shall be if He calls you that you shall say, 'Speak, Lord, for your servant is listening'." It took Samuel several times to recognize that God was speaking to him. **Who do you have in your life to help you discern God's voice?**

4. I complained to my father that maybe I needed to join a different church. He commented that the church wasn't the problem. He encouraged me to read and study the Bible to increase my knowledge. **In addition to attending church services, how do you increase your biblical knowledge?**

5. My Christian experience goes back to when I was ten when my grandmother picked me up to attend church with her. **What is your earliest or most memorable church memory?**

BIBLE STORY

People from all walks of life have shared stories of hearing God's voice or believing God called them to do everything from being in fellowship with Him to becoming a pastor and everything else in between. In fact, on the first anniversary of my mother's death, I experienced God calling me to Him. There would be other occasions when I recognized God's presence and voice. But, in this first instance, God connected me to my mother in a way I never expected.

Paul's conversion story is one of the most referenced stories of hearing or experiencing God's voice. Acts 9:17, "So Ananias departed and entered the house, and after laying his hands on him said, 'Brother Saul, the Lord Jesus, who appeared to you on the road by which you were coming, has sent me so that you may regain your sight and be filled with the Holy Spirit'." In this verse, Saul's physical sight was restored, and his eyes were opened to following Jesus. Saul, later known as Paul, became one of the most prolific writers of the New Testament.

In Philippians 3:5-6, Paul notes that he is a Pharisee from the tribe of Benjamin, and before his Damascus road encounter, he persecuted Jesus' followers. Immediately after his Damascus road experience, he was on fire for Jesus and shared the good news with everyone he met. He devoted the rest of his life to spreading the Gospel. He traveled, discipled others, and established churches. Paul has one of the greatest "coming on Christian experience" stories. Paul is inspirational for so many reasons, but the one that personally resonates with me is how Paul lived a life in direct opposition to Jesus, yet Jesus called him for a greater purpose. I hope you see the hope and grace in Paul's story and recognize that no matter where you are today, God can call you for His greater purpose.

God interacts with us all differently, so don't concern yourself if you don't have a specific story or instance where you felt God talked to you.

The most common way we hear God's voice is through hearing the preaching of His Word. Romans 10:17, "So faith comes from hearing, and hearing by the word of Christ." If you're not active in a local church, I recommend finding a church that teaches biblical doctrine and has a strong women's ministry that focuses on spiritual growth. I'm confident your faith and relationship with God will grow when you do. I also suggest devoting quiet time to God. Find what works for you, such as journaling, meditating on Scripture, and reading and studying the Bible. These are all ways to "hear" God. Do not concern yourself about looking for or waiting for God to present Himself to you. Everyone is not meant to have a Damascus road encounter.

PERSONAL REFLECTION

Being in fellowship with God allows us to hear Him, especially through the preaching of His Word. Take a moment to consider how you focus on fellowshipping with God. Pray to God for the specific help you need. Remember James 4:2, "You have not because you ask not."

1. When have you felt on fire for Jesus?

2. How do you personally communicate with God?

3. What does it mean to you to be in fellowship with God?

4. What Bible passage helps you to feel closer to God?

5. Have you listened to a sermon that you believe was meant specifically for you?

CHAPTER 6

The Label I Never Expected

"Now she who is a widow indeed and who has been left alone,
has fixed her hope on God and continues in entreaties and
prayers night and day."

. . .

1 TIMOTHY 5:5

A year had passed since I had filed for divorce and my emotions were on overdrive. I wanted to call Jerry. He occasionally reached out to me to say hi. On the day of our anniversary, I contemplated calling him if he didn't call me. For some reason, I wanted to reminisce about the happier times of our life together. Deep down, I knew it would only hurt me about living in the past, so I went to visit my father instead.

I sat across the kitchen table from my father, sobbing, barely able to speak. His eyes never met my tearful gaze. He concentrated on the puzzle book before him. Slowly, he drew a line to mark the word he had just found. Pleased with his success, a modest smile emerged at the corner of his lips. I continued to cry.

He remained silent for what seemed like forever. Then, when he finally spoke, he reminded me that I wasn't the first person to get a divorce and that I would not be the last. He continued to say, that it's been going on since the beginning of the world. Lastly, he reassured me, "You're hurting now, but in time you'll heal." He never coddled me, so his words didn't surprise me. In fact, I expected some hard truths from him. I nodded in agreement, sat up straight, and wiped my tears. We chatted for a while before I went home.

Four days later, I received a call from one of Jerry's best friends. I hadn't talked to his friend for some time, so it surprised me when I saw his name displayed on my cell phone. Jerry and I had been divorced for a year already, and I couldn't imagine what he wanted. In fact, it never dawned on me that it would have anything dire to do with Jerry. He didn't waste any time, "Tika, I don't know the last time you talked to or saw Jerry, but he isn't looking good."

"Wait, what? What are you talking about?"

"He's at Henry Ford Hospital in Detroit. I don't know about these things, but I think you better go see him."

A lump formed in my throat; I exhaled and then thanked him for calling me. I sat in shocked silence for a while and then decided to call my sister-in-law. After she confirmed that he was, in fact, very sick and in the hospital, I called his aunt and asked if I could come to see her even though it was late. Once I got her approval, I got dressed and drove the five minutes to her house. I broke down as soon as she opened the door. Crying, I asked for more details about Jerry's situation. She informed me that Jerry had been diagnosed with fatty liver disease. I assumed it had something to do with his alcohol consumption, but she explained that the disease is a complication of obesity. I'm sure his drinking probably exacerbated the issue. His liver was badly damaged and not functioning properly.

He had been transferred to Henry Ford Hospital in Detroit, one of the preeminent liver disease specialist hospitals. I shared with his aunt that I had almost called him on our anniversary, and she told me that he had taken a turn for the worse and probably would not have been able to talk. She shook her head in disbelief as she shared with me the shocking details of how quickly his illness consumed him. According to his doctors, he had gotten an infection and barely made it through the night. I needed to see him. I needed to go to the hospital.

Though it was ten o'clock at night, she agreed to ride with me to Detroit. We talked about Jerry's situation the entire drive. I asked if his "girlfriend" was supportive and standing by him during his illness. It angered me when I learned that she barely visited him in the hospital. Even though Jerry and I were no longer together, it broke my heart that the woman he chose over me essentially abandoned him in his time of need. Incredulous, I blurted out, "Did she poison him?" In hindsight, I realize that question was baseless and dangerously accusatory. Yet, I wondered how something like this could happen to a relatively healthy forty-three-year-old man. I struggled to wrap my head around the news.

I had finally started to feel a semblance of peace after losing my mother and divorcing Jerry, but after the news of Jerry's health, dread filled my thoughts again. It would be some time before my faith and trust in God matured to a level where sickness no longer frightened me.

In desperation, I drove over the speed limit to get to the hospital as quickly as possible. Based on what his aunt and friend had told me, it sounded as if Jerry was near death. The last time, when I had driven over the speed limit to see Jerry, I wanted to catch him in the act. This time, I drove over the speed limit not knowing if it would be the last time I would ever see him.

When we arrived at the hospital and reached his room, it was well after midnight, and the nurses were trying to administer his nightly medication. He had looked up when I walked in, but he appeared agitated. He argued with the hospital staff and seemed to hardly notice me. I walked over to him and said that his aunt and I were there to care for him. I extended my hand, and he grabbed ahold of it. Holding his hand at that moment felt natural. I had known Jerry since we were fifteen years old, and we shared a special bond despite everything that had happened.

He continued to argue with the nurses and refused to take his medications because he worried they were trying to harm him. I assured him I wouldn't let anyone harm him. I pleaded with him to take his medicine to heal his body so he could go home. After some convincing, he submitted to my pleas. He remained wired and agitated, though. I asked him to rest. He needed the rest, and so did I. I reassured him, "I'm here. I'll make sure nothing happens to you. Go to sleep, and I'll be right here next to you."

I dragged a chair from across the room next to his bed, rested my head on the grab bar, and slept by his side. He tossed and turned all night, and between the two of us, we barely got three hours of sleep. Even though we were divorced, I still cared about him and his well-being. All night long, I worried about the outcome of his situation. Both his best friend and aunt had shared the details of his condition, but I wasn't prepared for what I saw.

Over six feet tall and handsome, Jerry's presence took center stage in any room he entered. He dressed sharply and had a great sense of humor. Although he was overweight, you barely noticed because of his other attributes. The big, strong, and handsome man whom I loved was gone. I had never visited anyone in the hospital whose physical condition had deteriorated like Jerry's. He had lost a significant amount of weight and hardly resembled himself. His physical changes took my breath away. I didn't want my shock to show on my face. I remained strong and resilient in front of him. I didn't want my dread to discourage his will to live.

Two doctors entered Jerry's room the next morning. Still sitting at Jerry's bedside, I stood up as they approached. They introduced themselves and asked if we were family. I responded, "yes." One of the physicians commented, "He's a bit better today, but he's a very sick man. Right now, we're focused on making him as comfortable as possible." Those words stung my heart, and I wanted to cry. I realized that I had just learned of Jerry's condition, but it seemed to me like they had given up on him. I immediately focused on solutions and asked about options to cure him. The doctor apologized to me several times but told me he wanted me to know the truth. He said, "Without a new liver, there isn't much we can do. A healthy liver can repair itself, but his liver is too damaged."

Unfortunately, he wasn't a candidate to receive a new liver because he had consumed alcohol within the last six months of his diagnosis. They reserved livers for individuals who lived a healthy lifestyle and who ultimately had the greatest probability of a successful transplant. I understood the rationale, yet the reality of his situation hurt. I still loved him and cared about him. I certainly didn't want him to die.

I asked more questions to try to find a solution to save him. Jerry and I made eye contact, and he mouthed to me, "Just leave it alone." I nodded in agreement and hurried out of the room. I didn't want him to see me cry. Jerry had been dealing with his condition longer than I had. Of course, he knew more about it than I did. He seemed resolved to his fate, but I wasn't there yet. I didn't want to accept that he was dying.

I walked to the end of the hallway and cried. I composed myself as best as possible, texted family members, and asked for prayers. I took a deep breath, then made several hysterical calls home to my father and brothers. I updated them on Jerry's condition and said that I was afraid for him. I shared how he looked physically, that his liver was failing, and the doctors said there wasn't anything else to be done. Devastated, I leaned on the wall for support until I stopped crying. After calming down, I wiped my tears and returned to his room. I told him I had to go home and would return soon to visit him again. He nodded. We said goodbye, and I left.

Once I arrived back home, I got down on my knees and prayed. I apologized to God for getting a divorce. I asked if we were being punished because I broke our marriage vows and got a divorce. It wasn't that I was trying to "barter" with God, but I was willing to make a sacrifice that would be pleasing to Him to save Jerry. I did the opposite of what Matthew 7:7 teaches us, "Ask, and it will be given you; seek, and you will find; knock, and it will be opened to you." I now know that I should have just prayed directly to heal Jerry and that God doesn't work in if/then situations.

But in my limited knowledge, I prayed, "Lord, God if you save Jerry's life, I will honor my vows and restore my marriage." I prayed, "Give Jerry an opportunity to have a relationship with you. Give him another chance." I prayed more at that moment than I had in my entire life. It felt natural to pray for him. I wanted him to live, and to be healed. I didn't hate him. I had already forgiven him well before his illness.

A week after I visited him in Detroit, his family transferred him back to Grand Rapids, closer to home. One Sunday, while I visited him, I cared for him. I washed his face when we woke from a nap and fed him. He grabbed my hand, looked into my eyes, then leaned up to kiss me. He said, "I love you." I squeezed his hand and professed my love for him as well. We continued holding hands while I silently pleaded to God to heal him. I was hopeful. My church, the ladies in my Bible study, and my dad constantly reminded me that prayer changes things. I believed God would restore his health if I prayed and had faith.

When I returned to work the next day on Monday, I submitted a vacation request for the next Friday. I planned to spend the day with him and continue to comfort him. I wanted to spend as much time as possible caring for him. Sadly, I never got the chance to spend that day with him. When I woke up that Friday morning, I noticed I had a missed call on my cell from Jerry's aunt. My stomach dropped when I noticed the time the call had come in was 1:30 in the morning. I reluctantly listened to the voice message, knowing I would hear Jerry was gone. I broke down. I screamed angrily, "I was going to see him today! Why God?"

I lashed out at God. "What did I pray for?" "Why didn't You save Jerry?" I became angry with Him again for taking away someone I loved. I rebelled and stopped praying for several weeks. I was bitter and thought, what was the point of praying if He didn't answer? I tried to keep it together, and just push through as I've done in the past, but this time was different. I couldn't hold on this time around. I sought help.

Through my employee assistance program at work, I found a Christian counselor. On the first visit, he asked, "Tika, what brings you in today?" I certainly had a long list, but I told him my ex-husband had died. I sobbed as I shared with him my frustration about constantly hearing, "It's God's plan." He calmly responded that we don't know God's plan. And, even if it is God's plan, that doesn't mean it doesn't hurt.

YES. It does still hurt. I felt like his words allowed me to acknowledge that sometimes God's plan may be painful. His words meant the world to me. Until then, some well-meaning Christians unintentionally made me feel like I should be content because if it's God's will, I shouldn't cry or be sad.

I finally stopped crying and admitted to him that I was angry at God. He told me that God understands our humanness. That comment continued to make me feel seen and heard. I had six sessions with the counselor, and each one was more impactful than the last. He offered words that many of my Christian peers, although well-meaning, couldn't help me with.

A month later, on Halloween, I completely unraveled. I curled up on my bed in a fetal position and wailed at the top of my lungs. Halloween was Jerry's favorite holiday, and the thought of him not being able to enjoy it triggered sadness in me. A big kid at heart, he loved buying funny wigs or scary masks every Halloween. As fond memories started to flood my mind, while curled up on my bed, I screamed, "I can't take it anymore! Why! Why!" Then, as if out of nowhere, a Bible verse that a friend had asked me to read weeks earlier came to me. God presented himself to me yet again, this time answering my frantic pleas of "why" by giving me this verse which I heard as words being spoken out loud to me.

Job 1:21, "Naked I came from my mother's womb, and naked I shall return there. The Lord gave, and the Lord has taken away. Blessed be the name of the Lord."

At that moment, I thanked God for giving me both my mother and

Jerry for the time He had. That was the first time I thanked God for them. All the other times, I cried that they were gone. I thank God for my mother, for being the best friend I've ever had; for her laughter and fun personality. I thanked God for her common sense and ability to teach me valuable lessons I still follow today. I thanked God that she could stay home to raise my brothers and me and provide a loving, safe home. I thanked God!

I thanked God for giving me Jerry for twenty-seven years, for when we first met at age fifteen. I thanked God for the wonderful times we shared, our love, and even the bad times we experienced. I thanked God for the laughter and for the joy. I thanked Him for the memories I will forever have. I thanked Him for our love of travel, music, and movies. I thanked God!

Thanking God for my mother and Jerry gave me a new perspective on my faith journey. It felt like walking through a field of flowers and noticing the fragrant aroma for the first time. When you smell the flowers, you promise yourself that you'll always notice what is right in front of you from that moment on. I became more aware of what was before me and gave thanks daily. I understood that all belonged to God, and I was merely stewarding what was given to me for a predetermined time.

I found comfort and direction in 1 Timothy 5:5, "Now she who is a widow indeed and who has been left alone, has fixed her hope on God and continues in entreaties and prayers night and day." Even though Jerry and I had been divorced for a year, his death left a void in my life. I had to fix my hope in God by believing that I'd never be alone in Christ.

This verse encouraged me to put my faith and trust in God. I focused on rebuilding my life and soon began to recognize how my trust in God helped me to navigate in areas I never expected.

LIFE APPLICATION
Chapter Discussion Questions

1. Jerry had been dealing with his condition longer than I had, and of course, he knew more about it than I did. He appeared resolved with his fate, but I wasn't there yet. **How does God work in individuals to help them accept their fate?**

2. Job 1:21 "Naked I came from my mother's womb, and naked I shall return there. The Lord gave and the Lord has taken away. Blessed be the name of the Lord." **How can this verse help you to accept the death of loved ones?**

3. It wasn't that I was trying to "barter" with God, but I was willing to make a sacrifice that would be pleasing to Him to save Jerry. I prayed, "Lord, God if you save Jerry's life, I will honor my vows and restore my marriage." Out of desperation and fear, it's natural to try to "bargain" with God. Of course, God doesn't need us to do anything to receive his favor and mercy. **When have you been so desperate that you tried to bargain with God?**

4. Through my employee assistance program at work, I found a Christian counselor. Some church communities do not support seeking counseling assistance. **What is your opinion on Christians receiving professional help from a licensed counselor?**

5. At that moment, I thanked God for giving me both my mother and Jerry for the time He had. That was the first time I thanked God for them. All the other times, I cried that they were gone. This was an aha moment for me. **When have you had an aha moment that strengthened your faith?**

BIBLE STORY

Writing this chapter was surreal. Even though Jerry and I were divorced, he often texted to check on me. I appreciated his concern. Occasionally, I wondered and even hoped we would one day meet at a coffee shop to talk. I envisioned us greeting one another with a hug, sharing our feelings, and offering honest heartfelt apologies. At one point, we were the best of friends, and I believed we would reconcile our friendship, but not the marriage, though. Sadly, we never had an opportunity to meet at a coffee shop.

The realization of being separated from him in such a final manner was devastating. I never expected to be a widow, especially at such a young age. There are some individuals in the Bible who also experienced an unexpected label. Hagar, in the Bible, didn't deal with death, but she dealt with a situation in which she found herself with a label she never expected. Genesis 16:6, "But Abram said to Sarai, behold, your maid is in your power, do to her what is good in your sight. So Sarai treated her harshly, and she fled from her presence." Sarai was envious and jealous, and she treated Hagar harshly.

Just as I had thoughts of Jerry and me meeting for coffee, perhaps, Hagar had dreams for herself and her family. I imagine she was a young woman with a peer group. Maybe there was even a young Egyptian boy who made her laugh. But, she received the news that because she was Sarai's Egyptian slave, she would have to become a concubine and bear a child. Talk about an unexpected label!

As if things couldn't get any worse, Sarai was harsh to Hagar, and Abram didn't offer guidance to diffuse the situation. Unable to handle the harsh treatment, Hagar fled to the wilderness. Fleeing from our problems is a natural defense mechanism. Thankfully, an angel of the Lord found Hagar and ministered to her. Read Genesis 16:7-12 for specific details about when Hagar fled. After the angel of the Lord spoke to Hagar, she understood that God was with her. Genesis 16:13, "Then she called the name of the Lord who spoke to her, You are a God who sees." She received words of encouragement from the angel of the Lord. In dealing with her unexpected label, she understood that God hadn't forgotten about her and that He saw her. Amen! We all want to be seen by God. For reasons unbeknownst to us, we may deal with something in our lives that we never expected. I pray that you seek God's encouraging words, either in the form of Christian counseling or in your quiet time with God.

PERSONAL REFLECTION

We strive for greatness, make plans, and set goals. We have envisioned the life we want. Yet, unbeknownst to us, God may give us an unexpected label. Take a moment to consider your unexpected label. Pray to God for the specific help you need. Remember James 4:2, "You have not because you ask not."

1. When have you hoped for a specific scenario to occur in your life, only to have your dream upended by an unexpected label?

2. What unexpected label did you receive?

3. How did you manage?

4. Did you flee like Hagar?

5. Did you know God sees you?

CHAPTER 7

Trip of a Lifetime

"For I know the plans that I have for you declares the Lord,
plans for welfare and not for calamity
to give you a future and a hope."

. . .

JEREMIAH 29:11

I stared out the window as the plane taxied on the runway until it took off. Once the plane was high above the clouds, I sat back, reached for my bag under the seat in front of me, and grabbed my iPad and *Essence* magazine. I exhaled a joyful breath. Giddy and gleeful, it wouldn't be long before I arrived in Las Vegas for a solo vacation to celebrate my forty-fifth birthday. Never in a million years did I think I would ever take a leap of faith and go on a solo vacation. After years of endless tears and anger, I felt like I had finally transitioned into a positive and happy existence.

It took some time to reach this level of giddiness. I went on my solo vacation three years after my divorce and my mother's death and two years after Jerry's death. However, looking back, to get to this level of happiness, I had to handle the sale of the house I owned with Jerry. Had this not happened, I would've never achieved the independence to take this trip.

Finalizing the sale of my house almost didn't happen. My calls and text messages to Jerry had remained unanswered. I barraged him with calls to remind him of the closing date of the home we'd once shared. Less than a year before, my frantic calls to him had been pleas to come home or demanding to know his whereabouts. It was refreshing to no longer be concerned about his every move. Before, when he didn't answer my calls, it was because he had been with his mistress. I suspected he wasn't answering my calls this time because he was angry with me for "selling" the house. This shocked me because, at one point, during an argument, he yelled, "Sell it all. The house, the car, everything."

Even if he told me to sell everything in anger, I took it as marching orders. It felt surreal, but at the same time, it had to happen. Emotionally, our marriage had been over for years, and legally we indicated in our divorce decree that we'd sell the house and split the proceeds. Selling our home allowed us to enter the next phases of our lives. I remained resolute on what I needed to do to move forward with my life.

Determined to get to the next phase, I treated the sale of the house as a project plan. I wrote a detailed "to-do" list detailing out the tasks I needed to accomplish. The first two tasks were for me to meet with a realtor to start the process and to arrange a time for Jerry to meet with her to sign his portion of the seller's agreement. He complained and asked if I really wanted this to happen. I responded by reminding him that we were getting a divorce and the agreement had stipulated that we would sell the house. Begrudgingly, he signed the papers. I sighed in relief as his signing the seller's agreement moved me one step closer to my new life.

Our house was on the market only four days before we went under contract. A couple of months after we accepted the offer, we were scheduled to sign the final paperwork. The entire process moved along faster than either of us had anticipated. Jerry fumed with anger. I, on the other hand, saw it as a positive sign. We were no longer good for one another, and had it been drawn out any longer, I'm confident our situation would've escalated to a dangerous place. I found the rapid process to be a saving grace.

On my way to the closing, I checked my phone, hoping for a voicemail from Jerry saying he received my messages and would be there as scheduled. He did not leave me any messages. I let out a sigh of relief when I walked into the mortgage title office and saw Jerry sitting in the lobby. He sat with his arms folded across his chest and a scowl on his face. He glared at me as I grabbed a chair a few feet from him. *"At least he's here,"* I thought.

After ten minutes or so, the receptionist ushered us into the conference room. I entered first, and Jerry sauntered in behind me. It was a medium-sized conference room with a table that could seat six comfortably, but Jerry's anger made it appear much smaller. He breathed angrily. The tension in the room was palatable. He tapped his fingers on the table and moved his head about his neck, much like a weightlifter pumping himself up to lift heavy weights. He continued to glare at me from across the table. Our realtor and the title closer looked between us as they took deep breaths. You could cut the tension in the room with a knife. The title closer introduced herself, placed ink pens in front of us, and asked for our driver's licenses. Jerry forcibly pushed away from the table and stormed out. I signaled to her that I would return shortly and chased after him.

He marched across the parking lot towards his car. I asked if he was leaving. He yelled that this wasn't what he wanted, and he was, in fact, leaving. He screamed that I was moving too fast. Dumbfounded by his words, I shook my head in disbelief and thought, *"Moving too fast, seriously?"* I had filed for divorce approximately two and a half years after first suspecting his infidelity. Up until then, I begged and cried and pleaded for reconciliation. I pleaded for his love. To suggest I was moving too fast was laughable.

I told him we couldn't stop the process now. I believed we would face legal trouble if we walked out on the closing. I didn't know for sure, but I believed there could possibly be legal ramifications if we didn't follow through on our commitment. Upon hearing that, he reluctantly agreed to return to the conference room. I let out another silent sigh of relief as I followed him to the conference room. I was ready to get on with my life, and the house was my last connection to Jerry.

After I filed for divorce, I felt like a prisoner living in our home. Even though Jerry moved into his mistress' house, he still showed up and let himself into our house whenever he wanted. Unfortunately, I couldn't change the locks because he co-owned the house. It irritated me beyond words. I asked if he could give me a heads-up instead of showing up unannounced. Of course, he continued to do whatever he wanted. The closing of our house couldn't come fast enough. I wanted off the merry-go-round of demanding common courtesy from Jerry and him continuing to ignore my requests. I knew that once I had my own house, he wouldn't be able to saunter in whenever he wanted. I felt anxious about the freedom that owning my own home would bring.

After the closing, I had thirty days to clean and vacate the house. I set a goal to get everything cleared out as quickly as possible. I tried my best to keep Jerry informed of my actions. He refused to discuss anything over the phone with me, so I communicated with him via text messages to avoid arguments. Despite his angry demeanor, he no longer triggered negative emotional outbursts in me. The dynamics had shifted to me being more level-headed and Jerry being consumed with anger.

I prayed for the strength to leave Jerry. Not only did He answer that prayer, but God also strengthened me in areas I hadn't anticipated. I no longer desired to argue with Jerry, and I wasn't obsessed with the fact that he was living with his mistress. Instead, I remained focused on what I needed to do to get on with my life.

As I worked to vacate the house, I reminded Jerry to gather his remaining belongings. I shared with him the days I would be gone so we wouldn't have to interact. I asked what possible keepsakes or items he wanted as I planned to donate what we didn't want to Goodwill. I hired a few guys who agreed to take any remaining items in the house to the city dump. I managed to clean out our marital home two days before the thirty-day requirement. Relieved and exhausted, I notified the realtor that the buyers could take possession as scheduled.

I drove away from our house for the last time with my Jeep filled to the brim with clothes and household items. The rear window view was completely obstructed; thankfully, I only had to drive five blocks. After what seemed like forever, my new life had finally begun. With the help of family and friends, I moved into my new home. It was a ranch-style, three-bedroom house. It had a huge backyard, which was a plus because I retained custody of our three dogs, Furby, Zulu, and Samson.

Although I was thrilled to finally not have Jerry walk in on me, I also felt a tinge of fear. I had never lived on my own before. I went from living in my parents' house to living with Jerry. Thankfully, I didn't have much time to worry about it as I did my best to stay busy to make a home for myself. I had kept our bedroom furniture, a couple of folding chairs, and a treadmill, but other than that, I had to start completely over with new furniture and other household items. After I got off work, I visited furniture stores, took pictures of furniture, and asked about payment and credit options. To my surprise, some stores didn't offer payment plans. I quietly walked out of those stores as I had the sole responsibility for furnishing an entire house, and I had to be mindful of expenses. Nevertheless, I had fun window shopping until I made my first purchase.

After a few months of research and saving money, I purchased furniture for the main living spaces, and eventually, I completed the house with various decorative items like artwork, plants, lamps, and knickknacks. I loved my home. I hosted an Easter dinner for my family a year after moving into the house. My heart was full of joy as I watched my nieces and nephews running around and playing in my home. My dad and brothers commented how they were proud that I didn't let life get the best of me. Their words meant the world to me, especially because there had been a time when I doubted my own abilities. I remember at one point during the struggles of my marriage saying out loud to myself, *"I can't live without Jerry."* Now, I was thriving as a single woman. I often shook my head in joyful disbelief. Had I known I would be happy on my own, I would've filed for divorce sooner.

I had survived the first year living on my own. I skipped and jumped for joy as I walked through my house. I searched online for artwork with Jeremiah 29:11, "For I know the plans that I have for you declares the Lord, plans for welfare and not for calamity to give you a future and a hope." I finally found one I liked, ordered it, and hung it on the wall near my kitchen table. Each time I sat down to eat, I looked up and read the Bible verse and reflected that God had a plan and purpose for my life. It gave me peace knowing that my life didn't end after my divorce. God had other plans for me to live in Him.

I owed it all to God. In my joyful skips, I recognized God's presence in my life. God had woken me in the middle of the night with the idea of purchasing a house. He gave me the courage to walk into the bank to ask about applying for a mortgage. Purchasing a house of my own and living on my own proved to be a major turning point for me.

It boosted my confidence, prompting me to venture out of my comfort zone. If God gave me the courage to purchase a house on my own, what else could I do through Him? Ecclesiastes 3:1 reflected how I felt at the time. It reads, "There is an appointed time for everything. And there is a time for every event under heaven." I believed it was time for me to identify where I fit in the world without a husband.

I remember the first time I went to a restaurant on my own. Normally, I ordered food, picked it up on my way home from work, and ate it in front of the TV, or I purchased fast food and ate it in my car. Then, one day I thought it'd be nice to dine out and have a glass of wine with dinner. I drove to a restaurant near my house. I felt fine driving there, but once I walked inside, it felt weird. The hostess asked how many, and feeling somewhat embarrassed, I quietly squeaked, "just one." It crushed me, and I immediately felt sad. I wondered if anyone noticed me dining alone and if they felt sorry for me. I rushed through my meal, asked for a take-out container to box up the leftovers, and drove home in tears.

I knew that I didn't want that to be my reality, so I challenged myself and kept dining at restaurants. It took some time before I felt secure and confident dining out alone. It helped that I often frequented the same restaurants. The wait staff started to recognize me and knew my favorite drink order. Strangely, it helped me to feel less alone. Eventually, I began to enjoy my own company. Like Ecclesiastes states, there is time for everything. Going to a restaurant alone may not seem like a significant event, but I had to experience it to grow; that alone time allowed me to recognize what I could accomplish independently. As I embraced that Ecclesiastes verse, I focused on building a new life for myself.

My old life revolved around Jerry. All of my goals, interests, and activities were intertwined with his. I had to challenge myself to set new goals, identify new interests, and engage in new activities. Since I had never been much of a social butterfly, I prayed to God for the courage to meet new people and form new relationships. I knew I wanted to be around people of faith, so I searched Google for a faith-based divorce support group. The local Catholic church hosted the one that seemed to work within my schedule.

Even though I'm not Catholic, I decided to join the group as I felt I could still benefit from its support. Ecclesiastes 4:9-10 tell us that, "Two are better than one, because they have a good return for their labor. For if either of them falls, the one will lift up his companion. But woe to the one who falls when there is not another to lift him up." Each meeting started and ended in prayer. We read Scriptures and shared our stories without judgment. I had no idea what to expect when I joined, but it was one of my better decisions. I'm still in touch with the ladies from that group, and we often get together for brunch or lunch. The friendship and support we provided one another were invaluable because we didn't have to walk our journeys alone.

As the support group helped me to heal from my divorce, I strived to grow closer to God. I attended church every Sunday, participated in a weekly Bible study, and volunteered to help with a group for girls ages eight to eighteen. We mentored them from a biblical perspective and taught them how to manage challenges at school, at home, with their friends, etc. The girls loved the meetings and often commented how their faith helped them become better sisters, daughters, and friends. I loved seeing the girls grow and mature from one year to the next. My faith matured just as much as the girls whom I mentored. With my faith on the right path, I decided it was time to get my health back on track.

I gained a lot of weight during my tumultuous marriage as I ate unhealthy greasy foods to manage my stress. I was ready to lose the weight I had gained – not only for my overall health, but I also wanted to purchase new clothes. I searched for group exercise classes online and stumbled upon a women's running group. I had run track in high school, but it had been years since I ran. I thought it would be fun to start running again. After I contacted the group leader, she immediately added me to their group chat and invited me to join them on Saturday mornings. I struggled those first few Saturdays, but I never stopped. I ran my first 5k race with them within six months of joining the running group. The ladies finished the race before me but remained on the route and cheered me on as I crossed the finish line. They high-fived me, and I excitedly jumped up and down. I received a medal that is still proudly displayed in my home office. Before I knew it, I had lost weight. I felt great and looked better than I had in years.

I reflected on my accomplishments and was thankful for the support I received in the divorce group. I appreciated how the ladies in the running group held me accountable for my running and health goals. These groups fulfilled important needs in my life, but I felt something missing. I managed to do a lot on my own, but I thought it'd still be nice to have someone to join me for dinner, a movie, or to hang out. Google had become a great resource for me, and I Googled making new friends after the age of forty. To my surprise, several Meet-up groups returned. I had never heard of Meet-up groups, but it intrigued me, and I researched the site more. I reviewed the different groups available but didn't find many that interested me, so I followed the online instructions and started a group for women who wanted to make new friends after the age of forty.

After I published the Meet-up group, I received five requests right away asking for more information. Soon after, I began to schedule dinner outings, walks, movies, and other events. The membership grew close to fifty women, but as it goes, approximately fifteen women participated in all of the activities I scheduled. A year into the group, I transitioned it to a book club after surveying the ladies' other interests. After two years, the administrative work to maintain the group became too much. I announced to the group that I would be stepping down and asked if anyone wanted to take over. Thankfully, one of the ladies and her daughter agreed to keep the group going. To my knowledge, they maintained it for a couple of years after I left. The group had served its purpose in helping me to be more social and to make new friends, many of whom I still speak with today.

I had finally found my identity after divorcing Jerry. It was a welcome change in my life, and I embraced and thrived in my new identity. I had a church family, a full social life, and a healthier lifestyle that included running. I had a new normal, and I liked it. My scars were still there; some hadn't healed yet, but I refused to stay in bed with the drapes pulled. My family commented that they loved how I embraced life and encouraged me to keep living life to the fullest. I heeded their advice and took my biggest leap of faith yet.

My forty-fifth birthday was just a few months away, and I wanted to do something fun to celebrate. I thought a trip would be the perfect way to celebrate, and I wanted to travel on my own. Just like dining alone, I felt I would need to prepare myself for the possibility that solo travel may be my new reality. I realized I would have opportunities to travel with my family or friends, but I didn't want to depend on them to travel with me. I had to figure it out on my own. I thought Las Vegas would be a safe place to try because there are so many touristy things to do. During my stay, I took full advantage of all of the options at the hotel spa, shopped, and of course, ate very well. I enjoyed the trip and wasn't concerned about being alone; when I returned from my trip, I posted the following on Facebook.

Thank you for all the birthday well wishes! My trip to Las Vegas was twofold; first, to celebrate my forty-fifth birthday, and second to see if I had the moxie to go it alone. I found the below quote a while ago, proving a tipping point for me. I had to force myself to stop waiting for the perfect situation and take full advantage of the situation I'm in. I hope this is the first of many solo trips—I discovered that it's not as scary as I thought, and I quite enjoy my own company. I hope you enjoy this quote as much as I do!

"Stop waiting for Friday, for summer, for someone to fall in love with you, for life. Happiness is achieved when you stop waiting for it and make the most of the moment you are in now." – Unknown.

This quote encouraged me to find happiness and fulfillment in my life as it is and not fall into despair and hopelessness, waiting for things or people that may not be a part of God's plan for my life. For instance, I certainly wanted a dining companion to join me, but I eventually found happiness in treating myself to a nice restaurant. It would have been comforting to have known the ladies before I joined the running group, but then I would've never made new friends. I believe that God had placed me exactly where I was supposed to be for His purposes, and it was my responsibility to recognize how God worked through me. This is exactly what I took from that anonymous quote.

I continued making new friends, engaged in new experiences, and enjoyed my own company. Just as I started to celebrate how wonderful things were in my life, my brother received a sobering diagnosis that again tested my faith.

LIFE APPLICATION
Chapter Discussion Questions

1. It took some time to reach this level of giddiness. I went on my solo vacation three years after my divorce, and my mother's death, and two years after Jerry's death. **How many years did it take for you to reach a level of peace, happiness, or giddiness after your trauma? Are you still waiting for peace and happiness?**

2. Even though Jerry had moved into his mistress' house, he still showed up and let himself into our house whenever he wanted. Unfortunately, I couldn't change the locks because he co-owned the house. **Have you experienced a situation in which someone felt they had access to you whenever they wanted?**

3. Ecclesiastes 3:1 reflected how I felt at the time. It reads, "There is an appointed time for everything. And there is a time for every event under heaven." I believed it was time for me to identify where I fit in the world without a husband. **What appointed time are you still waiting to come to fruition?**

4. Since I had never been much of a social butterfly, I prayed to God for the courage to meet new people and form new relationships. It's not easy, but sometimes we have to get out of our comfort zone to grow. **When have you prayed to God to give you strength to grow in areas that weren't necessarily natural for you?**

5. I realized I would have opportunities to travel with my family or friends, but I didn't want to depend on them to travel with me. I had to figure it out on my own. **How do you feel about doing activities on your own?**

BIBLE STORY

During the turmoil of marriage, I lost so many things. But, what stands out the most is that I lost being "chosen" as my husband elected to be with another woman. I imagine you may be able to relate. We want to be chosen as someone's forever life partner. When I lost being "chosen," my confidence, self-esteem, worth, and joy went out the window with it. Once I realized God had chosen me, my life changed for the better. Over time, I experienced first-hand how God restored my faith, confidence, worth, self-esteem, and zeal for life. There are many restoration stories in the Bible. In fact, Job's restoration story is a personal favorite.

Job 42:10-11, "The Lord restored the fortunes of Job when he prayed for his friends, and the Lord increased all that Job had twofold. Then all his brothers and all his sisters and all who had known him before came to him, and they ate bread with him in house." This verse resonated with me as my dad, brothers, nieces, and nephews ate Easter dinner at my house. My heart is always full when I reflect on that moment and how God restored me back to my family as the confident and nurturing woman that I had been before my divorce.

Both Job's and my restoration stories took some effort on our part. Job humbled himself when speaking with God and prayed for his friends. I prayed for strength to leave Jerry; unbeknownst to me, God gave me that strength and the courage to take the first steps of living without Jerry. Keep in mind that God doesn't require nor need our efforts to restore us or change our lives. However, I believe we have to take steps to change the trajectory of our lives. We have to be active in making the change happen.

I also want to remind you that restoration isn't always in the form of material things or finances. In my instance, restoration came in the form of stronger faith, confidence, new relationships, and experiencing life in ways I never had before. My restoration didn't happen overnight.

In fact, from the time I first suspected Jerry of being unfaithful until I went to Las Vegas was six years!

PERSONAL REFLECTION

During our storms, we may lose relationships we value, our financial livelihood, or even our health. Once the storm is finally over, we often pray that God will restore us. Take a moment to consider what you lost and what restoration means to you. Pray to God for the specific help you need. Remember James 4:2, "You have not because you ask not."

1. What did you lose during your storm?

2. What does godly restoration mean to you?

3. What steps do you need to perform for your restoration to begin? (Remember, God doesn't need or require it.)

4. How does your definition of restoration differ from God's?

5. Does God restore everyone? Why or why not?

CHAPTER 8

Three Weeks

"Go and say to Hezekiah, thus says the Lord, the God of your father David, I have heard your prayer, I have seen your tears; behold, I will add fifteen years to your life."

. . .

ISAIAH 38:5

I signed off my work computer, grabbed my belongings, and walked to my car. The sun shone brightly, and the leaves were vivid bursts of orange and yellow. It didn't get better than an autumn Michigan day. I looked forward to talking to my father about the weather and how we were lucky the temperature hadn't dropped yet. Once I settled in the car, I grabbed my cell phone to call my dad on my drive home, which I did every day after work. I looked forward to our daily chat. As soon as my father answered, I heard the concern in his voice. He didn't sound like his usual cheerful self. My mood instantly switched to match his somber demeanor. I took a deep breath and immediately thought of my oldest brother, Robert, who had recently been hospitalized from complications due to congestive heart failure. I wondered if this was the reason for my father's solemn mood.

I couldn't help but think of a prior conversation my dad and I had about Robert that occurred during one of our daily phone calls on my drive home from work. My dad announced he had bad news. His words caught me off guard, and I couldn't imagine the bad news. Afraid and worried, I peppered him with questions, desperate to know the information before he could tell me. When I finally took a breath, he interjected and said he received a call from the hospital notifying him that Robert was in a medically induced coma. He continued that he didn't know more details than he had just told me, and we had to get to the hospital as soon as possible to find out what had happened. His words left me speechless. I told him I would be there soon to pick him up. I felt numb as we ended our call. Tears streamed down my face as I drove to his house.

It felt like déjà vu driving home from work and having another melancholy conversation with my father. I suspected his mood had to do with Robert, and unfortunately, I guessed correctly. He shared that he and Robert had talked earlier in the day. Robert requested a family meeting at the hospital. I asked my dad if he knew the purpose of the meeting. He confirmed he didn't know any more than what he'd just shared with me. Then he instructed me to pick him up right away.

Hospital family meetings and bad news tend to go hand in hand. I tried to stay positive but had a bad feeling, especially since Robert had been in a medically induced coma just a week earlier.

In a mental fog of uncertainty, I drove to my dad's house. When I arrived, I saw my dad sitting on the front porch, but I wasn't surprised. He prided himself on promptness. Whenever I picked him up for an event, he never kept me waiting. As I drove to the hospital, I asked again if he knew anything more because I thought he might hold back information. I figured he didn't want me driving to his house in a panic. He reiterated that he didn't know anything else. He reminded me that Robert was sick and that we had to pray for his recovery. Then, he told me to concentrate on the road, and we'd pray together at the hospital.

I pulled up to the hospital and let my dad out at the front entrance as I parked the car. I met him after parking the car, and then we walked to Robert's room. When we entered, my niece, (his oldest daughter), our brother, and his wife were already there. Everyone was present, so we called my other brother in Maryland, and he listened on speakerphone while the rest of us stood around Robert's hospital bed. No one spoke as all stared at Robert. Everyone looked perplexed as we waited for him to tell us the reason for the family meeting. He made eye contact with everyone, then said that he had a long talk with his doctors. His heart could not be repaired, which meant his body would soon shut down.

His voice cracked, but he composed himself and said he wasn't going to make it. Then, he declared, "But I'm not scared." The room fell silent as we stared at him. His words took my breath away. Tears welled in my eyes. This time, he sat up straighter and repeated with more resolve, "I'm not scared, and I love y'all."

My big brother, my hero, just said he wasn't afraid to die. We didn't know then that he had more time to process his health and come to terms with the end of his life. For reasons unbeknownst to me, Robert refused treatment that could have potentially prolonged his life. He also kept his health problems a secret from everyone. I wasn't happy that he carried such a heavy burden by himself, but at the same time, I understood. I'd kept my husband's infidelity a secret. I was embarrassed and ashamed that my marriage was in shambles. I wanted to avoid judgmental comments and questions, and I didn't have the mental capacity to handle anyone else's expectations of how I should have responded to my husband's infidelity.

I assumed Robert's reasons were similar. Maybe he didn't want to have to deal with accusations about not quitting smoking and not changing his diet. Although our situations differed, I understood my brother's decision to keep some hard truths to himself. He did what he needed to get to a level of peace for himself and come to terms with his fate.

Robert's assertion that he wasn't afraid testified to his faith and trust in God. That level of peace and confidence can only come from the Lord. In the years after my mother's death, my dad, brothers, and I were all on individual faith journeys. Robert started attending church even before I made a commitment to do so. Then, nine months after my mother's death, he was baptized. His announcement surprised me as I had no prior knowledge of his desire to get baptized. Even though this happened during the early stages of my faith journey, I knew this would be the most important step in Robert's spiritual life. I praised God for Robert being baptized.

Thinking back, I couldn't help but wonder about the timing of his baptism. Robert received the sacrament of baptism nearly a year and a half before he called the family meeting to inform us of his fate. In my heart, I believe Robert began preparations for his eternal rest after learning of his health problems. Mark 16:16 reads, "He who has believed and has been baptized shall be saved; but he who has disbelieved shall be condemned." Whether his decision to get baptized helped him to manage his grief after my mother's death or if he decided after he learned of his failing health, Robert inherently knew to turn to God to be saved.

Jeremiah 24: 7 states, "I will give them a heart to know Me, for I am the Lord; and they will be My people, and I will be their God, for they will return to Me with their whole heart." His heart may have been failing, but God gave him a heart to know Him. I'm confident that God directed Robert's steps to come to Him.

There are countless ways we can become part of God's family. Some are born into Christian families. Others meet influential evangelists who bring them to the faith at some point in their lives. There are deathbed confessions. And, then, there are people like Robert and me whom God watched over during our suffering. My marriage crumbled, Robert's heart failed, and we both grieved the loss of our mother. 1 Peter 5:10 reads, "After you have suffered for a little, the God of all grace, who called you to His eternal glory in Christ, will Himself perfect, confirm, strengthen and establish you." Through my pain and grief, I learned to lean on God. My brother Robert learned to lean on God, as well. I developed a deeper understanding of God and what it meant to be in fellowship with Him. Robert also grew and he exhibited a level of peace that none of us expected. This was evident when I spent time with Robert on many visits before he died.

During those hospital visits, I loved on him with hugs and kisses. We laughed and joked together. He seemed so joyful, happy, and at peace. I remember feeling so blessed to spend time with him. Not many people have an opportunity to say goodbye to loved ones. I can't help but reflect on the story of King Hezekiah and how God gave him more time. Isaiah 38:5 "Go and say to Hezekiah, thus says the Lord, the God of your father David, I have heard your prayer, I have seen your tears; behold, I will add fifteen years to your life." God granted Hezekiah fifteen more years. He gave Robert three weeks more on earth after we learned he was dying. This wasn't a mere coincidence. When Robert was in a coma, I prayed to God to wake him. I remember praying; I wanted to talk to him again.

The coma was so sudden that I wanted more time with my brother. I never specified how much more time I wanted. Robert had already come to terms with his faith, but when God extended his life three more weeks, it gave me the peace I needed to come to terms with the end of his life.

At the end of those three weeks, Robert died peacefully. My emotions were all over. One moment I was inconsolable. The next, I praised God for three weeks. I thanked God for the opportunity to say goodbye and express my love. More than anything else, I rejoiced that Robert had been baptized nearly a year and a half earlier. He had given his life to Jesus, and while I certainly didn't want him to leave me, I found comfort in knowing that Robert would be with God for eternity.

Finding comfort in knowing that Robert would be in eternity was new to me. I hadn't expected to feel comfort after my brother died. It surprised me when I found myself praising God. When my mother and ex-husband died, I was angry with God. I stopped praying. I blamed Him for my pain. I hadn't yet learned to fully love, trust, and have faith in God.

So, when I found peace after Robert was laid to rest, I recognized that

I had reached a new spiritual maturity. The Potter had been working in me and repairing me. I thanked God for giving me three more weeks with Robert. I praised God for calling Robert to baptism. And, I rejoiced for all God had done in my brother's and my lives.

I desired to grow even more in my faith. I was thirsty for His Word, so I completed yearly Bible plans and read biblical commentaries to develop a deeper relationship with God. I thought that having complete peace about my brother and being able to celebrate his life was the peak of my spiritual maturity, but when my father became gravely ill, my level of faith surprised me.

LIFE APPLICATION

Chapter Discussion Questions

1. Hospital family meetings and bad news tend to go hand-in-hand. I tried to stay positive but had a bad feeling. **Have you attended a hospital meeting for a sick relative? What was the purpose of the meeting?**

2. Robert refused treatment that could have potentially prolonged his life. He also kept his health problems a secret from everyone. **Why do you think family members sometimes conceal their health problems?**

3. Robert's assertion that he wasn't afraid to die was also a testament to his faith and trust in God. He was fully at peace. **Have you experienced loved ones who were fully at peace with their fate?**

4. There are countless ways we can become part of God's family. Some are born into Christian families. And, then, there are people like Robert and me whom God watched over during our suffering. **How did you come to the faith?**

5. Finding comfort in knowing that Robert would be in eternity was new to me. I hadn't expected to feel comfort after my brother died. **Have you felt comfort after the death of a family member? Why or why not?**

BIBLE STORY

Robert and I sought the comfort of God after our mother's death, but as we strived to grow closer to God, we kept secrets. For Christians, keeping secrets is never a good practice, as deception is often shrouded in darkness and sin. I didn't have the wherewithal to know this then, but I thank God I know better now. One story of secrets in the Bible that we can learn from is Abram and Sarai. They kept the true nature of their relationship a secret from Pharaoh.

Genesis 12:11-13, "See now, I know that you are a beautiful woman, and when the Egyptians see you, they will say, this is his wife, and they will kill me, but they will let you live. Please say that you are my sister so that it may go well with me because of you, and that I may live on account of you." Abram assessed correctly how the Egyptians would respond to Sarai's beauty. They noticed her and praised her beauty to Pharaoh – then delivered her to Pharaoh and moved her into the palace. For a momentary feeling of "safety," they lied. Sarai had become the "possession" of Pharaoh, he could have treated her harshly, given her away to someone else, or done anything else he wanted to do to her.

As we trek down the path of secrets, it often interferes with God's will for our lives. Abram knew of God's plan to make him into a great nation (Genesis 12:1-3). Yet, he feared the Egyptians and convinced Sarai to lie about their relationship. Abram did what many of us do today; we deceive others out of fear. I lied about the drama in my marriage out of fear that others would ridicule me for my failing marriage. Robert kept his health a secret out of fear of judgment that he didn't change his diet and lifestyle.

Abram feared the Egyptians more than he feared God. By doing so, he risked everything that God planned for his life and ours. Thankfully, God intervened, and He struck Pharaoh with plagues. Pharaoh realized God had punished him for Abrams' deception, so he directed Abram and Sarai to leave and take all their possessions. Who knows how long they would have kept this secret and the additional sins they would have committed if God hadn't intervened? What may have happened to Sarai if He hadn't intervened?

I can't help but think about how we limit ourselves when we choose to walk in deception instead of the truth. I know that the truth is hard sometimes, and we're afraid of what others may think, but once the truth is told, we can finally move forward with God's will for our lives. I finally sought God after I sinned so abhorrently and wound up in jail, and my pleas to God changed my life for the better. When Robert shared the truth about his health, our family was able to spend the remaining weeks of his life with him. God will not move us to the next phase of our lives if we are living deceptively.

God already knows what we're dealing with. I encourage you to unburden yourself and verbalize your secret to God and pray for His deliverance from fear so you may live in truth and in His light.

PERSONAL REFLECTION

Sometimes we may think having a secret is easier, but keeping up with the secret may require us to continue in our deception of sins and lying. Take a moment to consider what being truthful and walking in the light of Jesus means to you. Pray to God for the specific help you need. Remember James 4:2, "You have not because you ask not."

1. **Have you held a secret that got out of control?**

2. **How did it make you feel?**

3. **How might your secret go against God's will for your life?**

4. **What would it mean to you to unburden yourself from your secret?**

5. **How will that help you to walk in the light of Jesus?**

CHAPTER 9

Jesus is the Gate

"I am the door; if anyone enters through Me,
he will be saved, and will go in and out and find pasture"

. . .

JOHN 10:9

My father was rushed to the hospital with a diverticulitis flare-up. He lost a significant amount of blood which dropped his blood pressure and caused him to pass out. I panicked and cried when he didn't respond. It seemed like hours, but the emergency doctors revived him in a matter of minutes. I laughed nervously when my father came to and asked what had happened. He had no memory of passing out.

His condition stabilized to the doctor's liking so they left to tend to other patients. While we waited for him to be admitted to the hospital, we prayed for God's healing grace. Then, he told me to be sure to get his Bible and bring it back to the hospital. He smiled and said that God is the only way, and he didn't want to miss a day spending time in God's Word.

After receiving a blood transfusion, the hospital finally admitted him. They couldn't say for certain, but the doctors informed us to expect him to remain in the hospital for at least a week. If his condition improved, he could be discharged sooner, but due to his age, they had no intention of rushing his discharge. My father seemed unphased. Admittedly, I had concerns, yet he comforted me through his faith by reminding me to pray.

When he wasn't sleeping or being wheeled away for a colonoscopy or other testing, he read his Bible. With no discharge date in sight, he realized that he would miss in-person church and asked me to live stream it on my cell phone. He often fell asleep during the sermon, but when he woke up, he asked me to fill him in on what he missed. It strengthened our already close relationship. I loved sharing the sermon highlights with him and discussing how to apply the message to our lives.

Soon, we didn't wait for Sunday and started listening to sermons I found on YouTube throughout the week. I loved spending time in the Word with my dad. When I became frustrated that the doctors didn't have the answers I wanted, my father calmly said, "Tik, it's not up to them anyway. God is in control." Then, he instructed me to find another sermon. His faith encouraged me. I nodded and did my best to follow his faithful lead. We continued to pray for God's healing grace.

After nearly four weeks in the hospital, the gastroenterologist team found the source of bleeding in his colon and "capped" it. On his last day in the hospital, our prayers changed to praise. Joshua 1:8, "This book of the law shall not depart from your mouth, but you shall meditate on it day and night, so that you may be careful to do according to all that is written in it; for then you will make your way prosperous, and then you will have success." My dad said he never had a doubt that God would work things out. No matter what he endured in the hospital, he continued to model faithfulness to *me*. I remember thinking I should have encouraged him, but he did all the encouraging even while being connected to hospital machines.

Once discharged, he recovered at my home. With the support of occupational and physical therapists, he worked hard to regain his strength. He walked the hallway in my apartment building while I worked. The occupational therapist worked with him to regain his independence, and soon, he started heating up his lunch when I ran errands.

The visiting nurses and therapist commented that they couldn't believe the progress he had made, especially for someone his age. He'd smiled, tapped his Bible, and commented that it was all God. And, that

God wasn't ready for him to leave just yet. He recovered well, and within a month, he returned to his own home.

Spending those four weeks in the hospital with my dad, I experienced true faith. There were days when I said I had faith, but I found myself worrying. I expressed my thoughts to my father. Lying in the hospital bed connected to machines, he encouraged me. He reminded me to pray and to trust God. He said that God was ultimately in charge. Then, he said, "Tik, I've lived a long blessed life. I'm not ready to go yet, but if it's my time, know that I've been blessed." I marveled at my dad's ability to handle his health crisis with complete faith and without one complaint.

Life returned to normal, but then a year later, my dad was rushed to the emergency room again.

My father seemed to be unexpectedly tired three days after being hospitalized for another diverticulitis flare-up. I was alarmed by this because, just the day before, we had been talking and laughing during my visit. When I mentioned it to the nurse, she responded that his body had gone through a lot in a short period of time, and he needed the rest. While I agreed he needed to rest, I didn't like seeing him lying in a hospital bed, even if he was sleeping. I watched him sleep for a while, then pulled out a book to read that I had brought along with me.

The hospital room was quiet, with the exception of the few beeps from the IV drip and blood pressure machines connected to him. Suddenly, I heard him talking in his sleep. The words startled me. At first, I wasn't quite sure if I heard him correctly, so I leaned in closer and heard him say, "I come into this gate, and I won't lie." I held my breath. Did he really say what I thought he said? I turned on my phone to record his words and listened intently. A shiver went down my spine. I had heard him correctly. Stunned, I sat for a few minutes trying to gather my thoughts. I placed my hand on my heart as my mind immediately thought of John 10:9, "I am the door; if anyone enters through Me, he will be saved and will go in and out and find pasture."

I held my breath and said to myself, Jesus is the gate. Throughout my faith journey, God presented Himself through various signs that strengthened my faith and assured me of the path He prepared for me. So, when my father uttered those words, I knew it was a sign from God.

I don't know if my father, who appeared unusually tired, initiated the conversation with Jesus, or if Jesus called my father to come home. What I did know at the time is that Jesus is the gate. And when my father repeated over and over, "I come into this gate, and I won't lie." It became apparent to me that Jesus was calling him home. My father was a man of faith, and his words were not coincidental. I decided I needed to talk to my brothers.

My hands trembled as I texted my brothers to tell them what I heard our father saying. After texting them, I snuck out of my father's hospital room. I didn't want to wake him and disturb his conversation with Jesus. I grabbed my belongings, ran to my Jeep, and drove straight to my brother's house. Once my brother opened the door, I immediately collapsed in his arms, and he held me up as my legs buckled under me. I cried and rambled, "Jesus is the gate, Jesus is the gate." I was hysterical, pacing, rambling, and waving my arms about. He shushed me and told me to calm down.

He told me to stay at the house while he drove to the hospital to check on dad. The doctors were in my father's room when my brother arrived. They shared with him that his liver levels were low and that they were monitoring him. When my brother returned home, he explained to me what the doctors had told him.

Hearing the news about his liver confirmed what I had been thinking but hadn't shared with my brother yet. I believed my father felt his body shutting down, which is why he was talking to Jesus. I was absolutely convinced he was talking to Jesus about his eternal rest. I resolved to follow his lead. I stood up again, waved my arms about, and exclaimed that we must follow our father's lead. We must pray for a smooth transition.

This meant being in accord with our father by praying with him to enter the gate in peace. I was accustomed to praying for miraculous healing, but that wasn't what my father's words were pointing to, as he certainly wasn't saying that to Jesus. My father was resolved that he was ready to enter the other side. I wanted to honor his wishes and pray in agreement with him. I prayed mightily for him to enter the gate in peace. The Potter was working in me and repairing me.

Just two days later, my father went home to be with Jesus. My heart broke, and I sobbed uncontrollably. In the hours after his death, I found comfort that he remained faithful to God to the very end. Matthew 25:23 brought me comfort during that time. "His Master said to him, well done, good and faithful slave. You were faithful with a few things, I will put you in charge of many things; enter into the joy of your master." My father was a faithful servant. He honorably fulfilled his role as a husband, father, and man of Christ.

I do not doubt that my father completed the work God assigned him. His last assignment was out of his devotion to his family. The nurses shared with my brothers and me how they heard him praying all night for his family before he died. My father cared for us from when we took our first breaths until he took his last. Genesis 49:28-29 reads, these words of Jacob, "He blessed them, everyone with the blessing appropriate to them. Then he charged them and said to them, I am about to be gathered to my people; bury me with my fathers in the cave that is in the field of Ephron the Hittite." While my brothers and I prayed for him to peacefully enter the gate, my father prayed for us as we remained here in the living. This is a testament to my dad's faithful leadership of our family. Not only did he teach us to be supportive of and care for each other, but he encouraged us to pray and to lean on God. That we were all in prayer for one another didn't surprise me. My father wouldn't have it any other way, and I am proud that he led us to live a loving, supportive, prayerful life. Yes, well done, faithful servant!

My father modeled faithfulness and trust in God, which taught me how to navigate life as a Christian. When I was sad about losing my mother, he shared a funny story and talked about how blessed we were to have her for the time we did. I followed his lead and shared my own personal story about my mom. When I brought up missing my brother, my father reminded me to thank God for giving us three more weeks to spend with my brother. So I followed his lead and praised God for the time we had with Robert. Unbeknownst to either of us, my father would direct me on how to navigate my first Christmas without him.

As Christmas approached just six months after my father died, I reflected upon a personal story that he and I shared that brought joy to me. Every year a couple of weeks before Christmas, my father would invite me to his house. We'd visit for a bit; then, he would hand me his Christmas list with the names of the seven great-grandkids. Next to each name, he indicated a dollar amount, and next to that, he wrote a Christmas card. Every year my instructions were the same, ask the bank for new bills, place them inside a nice Christmas card, and fill out the card on his behalf. Then he always said, "Now, Tik, be sure to pick out a nice card for yourself and sign it from me." It made me chuckle. I thought picking out my own card was the funniest thing, and I never bought one for myself.

Then on the first Christmas season without him, I found myself at a pharmacy picking up a few items. As I walked through the pharmacy, I spotted the greeting card section. As if my dad had led me there, I walked to the card aisle and found the "To daughter" Christmas card section. I stood there for maybe fifteen minutes crying and reading several cards. I thought of the closeness of our relationship and the card that my dad would've picked out for me if he could. I finally found one that I liked. I returned home, addressed the envelope to myself, signed it from my father, and dated it. Then, I placed it in a brand-new jewelry box that I had found at his house when I was cleaning after he died. This gesture felt more like a new beginning than an end to our relationship, and I will continue to follow his lead and purchase myself a Christmas card from him every year.

I know that I will look forward to this new tradition every year as it will keep me close to my father. The jewelry box isn't very big, and after a few years, I'll have to buy a larger box. I don't know if I'll reread the cards. What I am certain of is that the faith and love that my earthly father showed me is only a fraction of the faith and love my Heavenly Father lavished on me. That kind of love changes things. It changes people. It changed me. The Potter was working in me and repairing me.

Seeing myself now as someone saved by grace through faith, I became a new woman. Knowing this, I recognize that God is not done with me. My faith journey is lifelong, and God will continue to change me into the woman of God He's destined me to be.

LIFE APPLICATION

Chapter Discussion Questions

1. While I agreed he needed to rest, I didn't like seeing him lying in a hospital bed, even if he was sleeping. Most of us can relate to spending days and nights at the hospital with a loved one. **How have you maintained your faith when you've had to spend hours, days, and even weeks at the bedside of your loved ones?**

2. I leaned in closer and heard him say, "I come into this gate, and I won't lie." I've heard comments that say that sometimes individuals who are sick decide when they are ready to transition. For instance, some people wait to talk to a family member before they transition. **When have you experienced a family member who was ready to transition to eternal rest?**

3. I was accustomed to praying for miraculous healing. My father was resolved that he was ready to enter the other side. I prayed mightily for him to enter the gate in peace. **How do you know when it's appropriate to pray for a miracle or for a transition to eternal rest?**

4. The nurses shared with my brothers and me before my father died that, they heard him praying all night for his family. My father cared for us from when we took our first breaths until he took his last breath. Even though we are adults, my father continued to pray for us. **What is the role of Christian parents in caring for their children, no matter their age?**

5. This gesture felt more like a new beginning than an end to our relationship, and I will continue to follow his lead and purchase myself a Christmas card from him every year. **What tradition did you begin before a loved one passed that you still continue today?**

BIBLE STORY

My brothers often teased me for being a bit of a spoiled brat. I won't deny that being the baby girl of the family certainly had its privileges! No doubt, I was a daddy's girl. My father and I were extremely close, and I spent a lot of time under his tutelage. He never stopped offering life lessons and words of wisdom. I'm blessed to have a treasure trove of knowledge to draw from when I need it most.

The story of Zelophehad's daughters reminds me of how my father prepared me to navigate life and how I remained resolved to heed my father's direction to the very end.

Numbers 27:4-7, "Why should the name of our father be withdrawn from among his family because he had no son? Give us a possession among our father's brothers. So Moses brought their case before the Lord. Then the Lord spoke to Moses, saying, the daughters of Zelophehad are right in their statements." Zelophehad's five daughters, who were not married, stood bravely before Moses to advocate for their security and safety, and God agreed with them!

Zelophehad had five daughters who had not yet been married. I imagine he grew increasingly concerned about their future. Can you picture him meeting with other families in hopes of finding a suitable husband? Then, unfortunately, one daughter after another, no marriage offers. I'm sure he prayed for his daughters, but in the meantime, we have to assume he prepared them to navigate life.

During the summer months, I spent many hours sitting on the front porch of my father's house, seeking his advice and following his directions on how I should live my life. I bet the same happened with Zelophehad. I envision his daughters milling about the small kitchen preparing fish, bread, olive oil, and dates. Then finally, sitting down to a wonderful meal, they'd be listening to their father's wise words. Maybe he taught them important planting and harvesting skills. I'm sure he taught them about the importance of seeking wise counsel from tribal leaders. Perhaps, he repeated the inheritance laws to them and that, as daughters, they were not entitled to inherit land upon his death.

As the years passed and there was still no husband for his daughters, he probably made them promise to go before Moses and to petition before the Lord to receive his inheritance. Then, as he was dying with his daughters at his side, he made them promise again to petition before the Lord. One by one, they promised. Numbers 27:3, "Our father died in the wilderness, yet he was not among the company of those who gathered themselves together against the Lord in the company of Korah; but he died in his own sin, and he had no sons." The inheritance law was changed, and it offered protection for future fathers who had no sons.

God instructs parents to teach their children in the ways of God. I was blessed to have a father that took his role seriously and taught me how to petition and pray to God.

PERSONAL REFLECTION

What an absolute blessing to be a parent. Take a moment to consider how you can prepare the children you have now or those you'll have in the future. Pray to God for the specific help you need. Remember James 4:2, "You have not because you ask not."

1. What does it mean to you to be a Christian parent?

2. What specific life lessons do you want to pass on to your children?

3. How will you teach your children to pray and petition God?

4. How will you prepare your unmarried son or daughter to navigate life as a Christian?

5. How will you prepare your married son or daughter to navigate life?

EPILOGUE

My memoir spanned a period of thirteen years. As you may have imagined, I didn't include every event over those years. I focused on the situations when I felt God's presence – especially the situations where I recognized that if it weren't for God's grace, I would not have made it out of the storm. I also focused on the instances when my faith either waned or was strengthened.

Here is a brief follow-up on some topics I shared in my story.

Motherhood: It was devastating to close our adoption file. Yet, deep down in my heart, I knew it was the right thing to do. As much as I wanted to be a mother, I believe God placed me where I needed to be for a reason. I'm at peace with the path that He chose for me. After my mother and husband died, I had the capacity to be my father's caregiver. Without having to share my time with a child, I freely cooked, cleaned, visited, and shared the last years of my father's life with him. Nothing has given me greater joy than knowing that I spent quality time with my father. I wouldn't trade that time for anything in the world.

A couple of months after I closed our adoption file, I invited one of my cousins over to "shop" my nursery. I encouraged her to take whatever she wanted. She drove away with a car full of brand-new baby supplies. It filled my heart with joy that she found items to care for her new baby girl. I donated the remaining items to Goodwill. I'm confident a young mother felt blessed to find quality baby supplies at a low price.

Arrest: After much discussion and negotiation, I received a misdemeanor simple assault charge. What a relief! This meant that instead of a jury trial, I had to go before the judge. I cried the entire time I stood before him. I'm not certain how he made out my words as they were incomprehensible between my sobbing. He listened intently, though, to my remorseful and apologetic cries.

When I finished crying, he expressed belief in my remorseful words and felt assured that my actions didn't define me as a person. He then proclaimed how he read over my case and noted that I had worked for the same company for many years, had never been unemployed, had a master's degree, and hadn't even had a speeding ticket. Much to my relief, he placed me on unsupervised probation for two years so I did not have to report to a probation officer.

He said he would be remiss if he didn't offer stern words that I needed to hear. I remember it like it was yesterday. He leaned forward and stared directly at me, "You do realize that your husband may continue to see this other woman, and if that happens, you have to be a good girl and stay away from both him and this other woman." I nodded in agreement.

I thanked the judge and promised him he would never see me again! In conclusion, he assured me that he would expunge the case from my record if I were a good girl and did not get into any more trouble for the next two years. Talk about a sigh of relief. I joyfully ran from the courtroom to my car and listened to upbeat music on my drive home.

In addition to that fantastic news, I never appeared in the *Busted* magazine. The magazine listed the names and posted mugshots of recently arrested individuals. Every week for two months, I visited a local convenience store to purchase the latest edition. I held my breath each week as I searched through the names and pictures. Thankfully, I never appeared in that magazine. Whew! It had to be the grace of God.

Pets: We acquired the dogs early in our marriage, and they were quite old when we divorced. Sadly, over time, I had to put each of them down. Samson had cancer. Furby's health deteriorated, and he cried out in pain. Zulu stopped eating and lost weight. Losing a pet is extremely hard, so I gave myself time to heal after I put down the last one. After a year, I wanted to be a "mama" again, but being a single dog owner overwhelmed me. A friend had a kitten, and I absolutely loved playing with the kitten. I've never had a cat before, but I thought it would be a better option. I decided to adopt two four-month-old litter mates. I named them Sasha and Bella. They are complete heart snatchers and are an absolute joy in my life.

House: Since I no longer had dogs, I didn't need a house with a large backyard. Plus, it felt like a waste living in a house with rooms that I hardly used. I sold my house and moved into an apartment-sized condo. It's a perfect size. Plus, I love the freedom of not having to do yard work or snow removal.

Remarriage: The number one question I get asked more than any other question is, "Tika, do you want to marry again?" Smiling and shaking my head no, I give the same response, " I have not prayed to God to send me a husband."

Marriage has not been my focus. I experienced so much trauma over thirteen years that I barely had time to catch my breath, and there wasn't much time to even think about marrying again. Not only that, but I believe I needed to take the appropriate time to heal. It wouldn't have been fair of me to enter into a marriage when I wasn't mentally, emotionally, or spiritually healthy.

I don't know what the future holds, but when and if it's God's will, I believe He will place a marital spirit in my heart and will send a suitable Christian husband my way. For now, I'm fine.

Faith Journey: My journey continues. My bookshelves are overflowing with books! I love reading biblical commentaries to learn more about God's Word. I'm active in church and attend women's Bible study meetings.

I can't stop talking about and sharing God's Word, so I started a Christian and inspirational online channel to encourage women dealing with divorce, grief, and loss.

www.tikamccoy.com

ACKNOWLEDGMENTS

I was blessed to connect with many groups and associations who welcomed and supported me on my journey of healing. Their unconditional support and/or friendship helped to strengthen my faith in immeasurable ways. Thank you to the wonderful ladies in STARS- Sisters Taking Action Reversing Statistics; the wonderful men and women I met at the Catholic Diocese Divorce Support Group; the wonderful and fun ladies I had the pleasure to hang out with from the Grand Rapids African American Women's Meetup Group. I'd also like to thank the supportive counselors who listened to me and made me feel heard and seen at Pine Rest Christian Counseling. Through my father's advice, I joined the First Community AME Women's Bible Study Group. These faithful women encouraged me, prayed for me and were instrumental in helping me to increase my biblical knowledge. I can't thank everyone in these groups enough.

A year after living on my own, I recognized God's amazing grace in my life and started journaling and jotting down notes about how much He blessed me. I inherently knew I had a story to tell just after that first year post-divorce. Then, as my life continued to upend, I felt compelled to tell my story. I joined various writers' groups that provided invaluable feedback on my writing journey. I'd like to thank the Grand Rapids Writer's Exchange and the Midwest Writer's Group. I'd also like to thank Kelly O'Dell Stanley, who read the first ten pages and provided valuable insight and feedback. I would be remiss if I didn't thank Hillary

Koenig for her professional editing services. She ensured all the t's were crossed and i's were dotted. Thank you, Hillary.

To ensure my memoir was inspiring and relatable, I reached out to several individuals who agreed to be beta readers. Although busy with their own lives, they graciously agreed to read my memoir and provide invaluable feedback. A special thank you to Jean Mikula who provided suggestions to improve my story.

I'd like to extend a very special thank you to Stephanie Miller, my writing coach at www.butterly-beginnings.com. Stephanie did an amazing job coaching me to complete my book. She assigned due dates and scheduled touch-point meetings which kept me on task. Stephanie also helped me to organize all the notes, thoughts, and content I had amassed over thirteen years! Thank you, Stephanie!

My faith journey was not mere happenstance or coincidence. I know that God orchestrated specific people, situations, and things in my life for a reason. I don't have the words to explain how I would one day cross paths with someone who gifted me Bible commentaries, devotionals, and yearly reading plans. Who introduced me to Reformed Theology and scholars that provided the answers I needed to grow in my faith. Someone with whom I was able to comfortably discuss the goodness of God. I'd like to extend an earnest and heartfelt thank you to my spiritual mentor and one of my closest friends in Christ. Thank you.

ABOUT THE AUTHOR

Tika McCoy is a passionate Christian who finds joy in spending time with Jesus and delving deep into His word. Armed with a master's degree in Family and Consumer Science, she seeks to empower and support Christian women as they navigate the challenges of life after grief, loss, and divorce. McCoy's desire to uplift and encourage shines through her words, offering solace and guidance to those in need.

Professionally, McCoy excels as a corporate trainer, designing and facilitating training programs for new employees. Beyond her professional endeavors, McCoy finds joy in her role as a cat mom to Sasha and Bella.

When she's not immersed in her work or spending time with her feline companions, McCoy indulges in her passions for biking, traveling, and reading. Currently residing in Michigan, she also finds immense joy in observing and admiring God's awe-inspiring creations, including bees, butterflies, and hummingbirds.

Her memoir, *Broken Clay: Finding Renewal in the Potter's Hands*, reflects her deep love for God, her dedication to helping others, and her unwavering belief in the power of faith and restoration. Through her writing, McCoy aims to uplift and inspire readers, offering them a glimpse of the transformative grace that can be found in a life dedicated to Christ. Find out more about Tika McCoy at tikamccoy.com.